R J Green

Country planning
The future of the rural regions

Manchester University Press

© R. J. Green 1971

Published by
Manchester University Press
316–324 Oxford Road
Manchester M13 9NR

ISBN 0 7190 0455 1

ce

Printed in Great Britain by
Butler & Tanner Ltd, Frome and London

Country planning

Contents

List of maps, diagrams and plates

Acknowledgements

I wish to express my thanks to the County Planning Officers of Cornwall, Cumberland, Dorset, Northamptonshire, and East Suffolk, for permitting the use of various plans and reports to illustrate parts of the text: to the Editor of the Eastern Daily Press for permission to reproduce photographs of Thetford; to the County Planning Officer of Norfolk, who has always encouraged my academic aspirations; to David Robinson whose comments were both critical and encouraging; to Stuart Thompson, who drew the maps, and to Hilary Muir who typed the first draft.

1 Rural and conurban regions

> In the village there is always the illusion, that one can reach out and touch the past—it is there in the weathered walls of grey churches in living festivals and a way of life which is one of the most loved of English memorials.
>
> Martin, *The Secret People* . . . .

A nation of town-dwellers, we hold country life and country traditions in high esteem, and we regard the countryside as a natural phenomena to be protected against the economic and social pressures and demands emanating from the towns we live in. Country life is still seen by many as uncomplicated, and country values as direct and real, compared with the apparent sophistication and superficiality of town life. The belief still persists that close communion with the soil has some intrinsic value which makes farming a way of life morally beneficial to farmer and farmworker; and the village, both as a social institution and as a form of settlement, is seen as a monument to the great traditions of the past, of such significance that societies of well-meaning senior citizens are formed to preserve it from change. But the traditional function of the village, to accommodate people working on the land, and their dependents, and the simplicity for which its life is so much admired, seem largely to have gone.

A study group on living and working in the countryside for the second 'Countryside in 1970' conference[1] suggested that the

old patterns of country life are breaking up. Urban values are spreading their influence throughout rural areas and exert powerful economic and social pressures on the traditional forms of community life in the countryside. Expansion of the nation's population, increased mobility of the individual, demands of urban development on rural space, technological changes in industries and new methods in agriculture all contribute to the rural transformation which is now proceeding at accelerating pace in many parts of the country.

At the turn of the century the majority of rural settlements in England and Wales were still comparatively isolated and self sufficient. Their inhabitants were generally assumed to be politically and socially conservative, inward looking and economically dependent on the land. Two World Wars, universal franchise, state education, mass media of communication, mechanised farming and motorised transport have together broken down the isolation, changed the economic and social status of the village, and narrowed the gap between urban and rural attitudes so far that in some areas they can hardly be recognised apart. Indeed, life in most parts of the countryside has changed so much that the social and economic conditions of the 1920's would not be tolerated by most farmers, farmworkers or their families today. Mains water supplies, electricity, school buses, health services and transport (private if not public) are now generally taken for granted or demanded as of right. Most of these rural facilities are provided and maintained by central and local government or by the nationalised industries, and are subsidised by the urban community, through a system of grants, or fixed charges unrelated to the cost of the service.

Country life now seems to be distinguished from town life less by the attitude of the inhabitants than by the size of their settlements and what they can support by way of facilities and services. Yet many people, both in town and country, seem unwilling to accept this; the reality of the past has become a present myth, sustaining the 'demand' for an unchanged and unchanging countryside. Rural affairs sometimes seem to be directed more by emotion than by reason and country planning is no exception to the rule. Country planning has been, and in many counties still is, more concerned with defending the countryside against change than with the revolution which is changing the face of the countryside and which is undermining the social and economic structure of the villages whose fabric is being physically preserved. Rural planning policies have aimed primarily at maintaining the status quo, through the encouragement of infilling in villages, the prevention of sporadic building in the open countryside and by encouraging the establishment of small industrial concerns, in scale with the locality. Rural settlements have been classified into those whose aesthetic qualities merit preservation, and those which do not, and those with potential for expansion and those without. Potential for expansion has often been taken simply from a population growth trend, so that plans have generally added an element of preservation but without disturbing the established trends of growth and decline. In the negative sense that they have prevented development which might have intruded into the open countryside, and have encouraged building where it seemed to do least harm, rural planning policies have been moderately successful, but the 24 years since the Town and Country Planning Act of 1947 represent two decades of wasted opportunity for positive rural planning.

Rural planning policies have generally meant, in practice, the imposition of an *ad hoc* control of new development. A planning decision, by most local planning authorities, has depended on an assessment of what is called the individual merit of the application, determined as objectively as possible, but usually without the benefit of either a long-term strategy or a detail local plan. Little attempt has been made by local planning authorities to evolve policies, either to recognise the changing economic and social conditions in rural areas or to take advantage of the increasing physical and social mobility of the rural population. The present policies and practice of the local planning authorities will neither solve the problems of the more remote areas, where many of the settlements have a doubtful economic and social future, nor ensure that the development of towns and villages in growth areas follows a logical pattern.

In this book I have attempted a survey of country planning theory and practice, defining as the country, not only the open countryside, hamlets and villages, but also the country towns in rural areas outside the conurbations and industrial regions. In making this distinction between the rural and conurban regions, pockets of countryside are isolated within the conurbations, while some large industrial towns and cities are defined within the rural regions. Thus country planning is not exclusively concerned with agriculture, forestry and villages, just as planning in the conurbations is not exclusively concerned with large-scale urban problems. The traditional concept of town and country no longer seems valid with a highly mobile population living in a highly urbanised society, but the distinction between the conurban and rural regions has meaning, if for no other reason than the difference in intensity of economic and social activity, and in the consequent scale of the planning problems. Within the profession of town and country planning it is recognised that there are specialised skills applicable to the planning and management of the physical environment and that these are applied differently at regional and sub-regional, district and local scales. My contention is that there is a further distinction between planning in the rural regions and in the conurbations, not in the broad objectives of physical planning, but arising from the scale of operations, and from the different materials of which the rural and conurbation regions are made.

In any discussion of country planning, the point recurs that it is difficult to distinguish clearly between an urban and a rural community. For example, Norwich lies at the centre of a rural hinterland and may fairly be described as the administrative and commercial centre of a rural sub-region. Nevertheless, it is equally concerned with insurance and manufacturing industry, operating at national and international levels, and most of the nearby villages lost any resemblance to agricultural communities many years ago. These villages are occupied mostly by commuters, and justify being called villages only by the scale of services they provide and by being set in the midst of agricultural land. As the distance from Norwich increases the commuter element generally decreases. Even so the more remote towns and villages have a closer affinity with the regional centre than Norwich has with a major urban and industrial complex such as Merseyside, Tyneside or Thameside. A truer division between urban and rural seems to lie at a regional level, between rural regions and conurban regions, in their social, economic and demographic characteristics and problems, and in the planning policies applicable to them.

The boundary between the rural and conurban regions cannot be drawn as a single line, because the character of the one gives way to the other over a transitional zone, some five to ten miles wide, ten to fifteen miles out of the larger urban concentrations. This differentiation places the main urban commuter zones within conurban regions, but leaves the regional and sub-regional centres within the rural regions. There are conurban regions in lowland Scotland, in a vast arc round the southern end of the Pennines, in South Wales and the Bristol area, and in South East England. These conurban regions are separated by the irregularly shaped tract of rural Britain, which at present divides into six rural regions: North Scotland; South Scotland and North England; East of England, including East Anglia; South central England; South West England; and Wales and the West Country (Map 1).

In England and Wales some 60 per cent of the land area, but only about 17 per cent of the population are within the five rural regions. And of the eight and a half million people living within the rural regions, in England and Wales approximately 250,000 live in the City of Plymouth, approximately 1,380,000 live in 14 towns and cities of between 70,200 and 150,000 population, 740,000 live in 15 towns and cities of between 35,000 and 70,000 population, 670,000 live in 29 towns and cities of between 15,000 and 35,000 population, 840,000 live in 80 small towns of between 7,000 and 15,000 population, and over four and a half million live in smaller settlements.[2]

Thus a substantial minority of the population still live in a large number of relatively small country towns, villages and hamlets. A great many of these settlements have populations of less than 500 persons. The rural regions may be distinguished from the conurban mainly by the dispersed character of settlement, by the lower population densities, lower scale of growth, and lower levels of investment (particularly if expenditure on inter-conurban communications, power for national consumption, and defence are excluded).

At the 1969 Town and Country Planning Summer School,[3] in a paper with the rather frightening title 'The spatial organisation of hyper-urban societies', Lionel March[4] described the results of some studies based on the present distribution of population in England and Wales, and on long term projections, based on recent trends and somewhat more sophisticated mathematical models. Using the 50 kilometre grid, Mr March suggested that a distinction could be drawn between grid areas with more than 1·5 per cent of the population, and those with less. The grid areas with more than 1·5 per cent of the population coincide roughly with the conurban regions, and the grid areas with less population coincide with the rural regions. The projections suggested that the South Wales and Bristol, Midland (Pennine) and South Eastern conurbations would extend into the rural region which at present separates them in South Central England. Areas close to the motorways, such as Milton Keynes, seem the most vunerable, and the South Central rural region might become so fragmented that it would virtually cease to exist as a rural region in the sense that it is defined in this book. The result would be a vast conurban area—or series of overlapping conurbations—linking Merseyside, Humberside, the Midlands, London and the south coast, and Bristol and South Wales, with intermediate rural areas, possibly in mid-Kent, the Salisbury Plain, north Dorset and in the Derbyshire Peak (Map 2).

When the economic planning councils were established in 1965, the standard regions, which had first been defined for civil defence, were adapted to form the economic planning regions. With some modifications, these regions were again adopted by the Royal Commission on Local

Government in England,[5] as the basis for their suggested provinces. These Provincial Councils

should each cover an area of the country where there are major issues that ought to be considered together . . . its various parts should be economically and geographically linked; and its work will be made easier if there exists among its inhabitants a sense of provincial identity, rooted in history, economic traditions or geographical facts. Our investigations suggested that the present eight economic planning regions not only provide areas of suitable size for the functions of provincial councils, but also reflect such sense of provincial identity as exists in various parts of England. . . . The proposed provinces, therefore, depart from the boundaries of the present regions only where there would be clear advantage in their doing so. One of the biggest differences is that the northern economic planning region becomes the north-east province, Cumberland and Westmorland joining the north-western province and most of the North Riding forming part of the Yorkshire province. Another is the inclusion in the south-east province of most of Northamptonshire, now in the East Midland economic planning region. There are several other instances where provinces diverge from economic planning regions. In each case examination convinced us that the change would help associate areas which had common problems in one province.[6]

The economic planning councils were not charged with the specific duty of preparing strategic plans for the location of physical development and growth, but, as the report of the Royal Commission stated, economic and physical planning are so closely related that it is impossible to plan the one without considerably influencing the other. There is a strong thread of physical planning running through each of the studies published by the economic planning councils. The Provincial councils, as proposed by the majority of Commission members, would have a specific duty to prepare a provincial plan, for

the changing distribution of population, migration to and from a province, the location of new major growth points, the large scale movement of people from one unitary[7] or metropolitan area into another, the broad divisions of the province into urbanised, agricultural and recreational areas, major industrial developments with their implications for employment, housing and transport, the provincial pattern of road and rail communications, the siting of airports, the future of seaports, and the siting of new universities and of cultural and sporting facilities serving a wide area.[8]

A comparison between the conurban/rural regions and the 'economic planning' regions suggests that an objective assessment of rural economic and planning problems in many regions has been prejudiced by the arbitrary sub-division of rural regions by the boundaries of the standard regions, and the inclusion of parts of the rural regions within the adjoining conurban regions. An example of this is afforded in the East Midlands study, which, quite correctly, concentrates on the industrial and conurban problem of Leicester and Nottingham, but to the virtual exclusion of any serious discussion of the rural areas to the east. Only East Anglia and the South-West economic planning regions are predominantly rural. Scotland, the North-East, the North, the East Midlands, and Wales contain large conurban areas, in which most of the population is concentrated, but each region also contains a substantial rural area. Only the South-East and the West Midlands are almost exclusively conurban (Map 3).

Similarly, some of the provinces envisaged by the Royal Commission on Local Government in England would be predominantly conurban in character, but with a substantial rural population as a minority, whose interests will be subordinate to the conurban majority. The interdependence of town and country is an underlying theme of the Royal Commission report, and there can be little argument with this so far as local or sub-regional links are concerned, but it seems to have less meaning when applied to the major conurban and rural regions. The proposed provinces would split the conurban regions by boundaries across which there are strong economic and social links, and would combine the parts of each conurban region with the adjoining rural area, thus compounding the error by dividing rural regions which would benefit from comprehensive provincial plans (Map 4).

The Labour Government excluded the proposed Provincial Councils from its programme of Local Government reform, the white paper issued in 1970,[9] explaining that the idea was deferred rather than rejected, and that it would be re-considered when the report of the Commission on the Constitution had been received. At the time of writing, the present Government has not made any formal proposals for local government reform, and its attitude towards Provincial Councils remains uncertain. In *Wales—the Way Ahead*,[10] a realistic sub-division was made which recognised the industrial south and north east, and the more rural areas of north west, central and south west Wales. Serious consideration should be given to defining separate conurban and rural regions, as a basis for provincial or regional councils for the whole country[11] (Map 5).

B

The Labour Government accepted the majority recommendation of the Royal Commission, that the present system of County Boroughs, Administrative Counties, Districts and Parishes should be replaced by large single all purpose authorities. In a minority report, Derek Senior dissented from the majority view and suggested that a two tier system of local government should be retained, but based on a series of 'city regions', designed to link each major town with its surrounding rural hinterland. Again, at the time of writing, the new Government has not published its proposals but it is thought to be in sympathy with the principle of two tiers of local authorities, at least in the rural regions.

Before the development of motorised road transport, towns were usually surrounded by an area of cash crop and market garden production. Writers on the urban utopia, like Ebenezer Howard, usually included in their diagrams of the ideal town, a market garden zone, resembling an early form of green belt. Greater specialisation in horticulture marketing, on a much larger scale, and the partial replacement of fresh foods by frozen and canned, have largely removed the close relationship between the town and the surrounding agricultural land. Links between the town and its hinterland are now less concerned with the marketing of produce and the interchange of goods and animals, and more with the use of the facilities of the town by people living in the country, and with the extension of the urban labour market into the surrounding countryside. The concept of the city region or sub-region is based on this double sphere of influence—employment and service—and the system of public and private transport needed to sustain it.[12]

The rural regions defined on Map I contain a series of city regions and sub-regions, and many planners regard these centres as places to concentrate future growth. In the major centres, a variety of inter-related industries can be developed, supported by the technical skills and training facilities of 'local' universities and colleges, and served by a relatively large pool of highly skilled labour. For much the same reason, the city region is suggested as a basis for new local government and planning areas; the combination of the city with its region may be a means of ending the fratricidal warfare between town and country, or more particularly, between city and county councils, which has bedevilled planning for very many years. Whether this city-oriented concept of local government would be beneficial to either the countryman of today or to those people who, in the future, choose to live outside the major towns and cities is much less certain. The urban justification for the city region is clear; the city can seek the solution to its growth and renewal problems in the surrounding countryside far less restricted by rural protest. The rural side of the balance sheet is much less clear; possibly some influence on the provision of urban facilities, but if rural affairs are to be dominated by city politics, the countryman must feel a much stronger stake in the life of the city than he would obtain through his councillors having a vote alongside their urban colleagues. The farmer no longer depends on local markets to sell his produce and although his future neighbours may work, shop and play in town, there is no guarantee that they would willingly exchange more direct control of rural affairs for a shared control of urban and rural affairs through a city regional council. Certainly some form of cohesive local government should operate in the rural regions to remove the present conflict between county and city, but the city region seems to imply far too much social and economic dominance by a single city and its centre. The Royal Commission on Local Government in England noted that in some areas such as the south-west, the city region seemed to mean creating artificially constructed areas whose people have no sense of looking to a city centre or of sharing interests peculiar to themselves. Looking generally at the rural regions, the larger unitary authorities should have a greater chance of success in holding the delicate balance between town and country interests than the smaller city-regions.

2 Mobility in the rural regions

The view is still heard that the major urban areas, or conurban regions, are more active, and more responsive to new ideas, than the rural regions. There may be some truth in this contention, but the rate of social and economic change in the rural regions is increasing fast, and a rural situation is no longer synonymous with outdated thinking or with a static society. Most social and economic changes have some relevance to planning, but the town and country planner wishes to identify those aspects of change which are manifest in some identifiable physical development. Thus, changes in social class, status and kinship, which seem to attract special attention from both urban and rural sociologists, are largely ignored by town and country planners. Similarly, economic changes such as increasing productivity, collective bargaining, union reform, or reorganisation of management, are considered very much less relevant than changes in employment structure, investment levels and other phenomena more clearly related to demands for new buildings and extra land. In the rural regions, the aspects of change which seem most relevant to planning are:

(a) greater affluence, by which the demand for new houses, shops, roads and other paraphernalia of town and village life, is stimulated;

(b) the mass media of communication, seen as one of the main reasons for the increasing standardisation of demand, and the disappearance of what little remains of regional differences;

(c) higher standards of education, apparent in more, and larger schools, and new and larger polytechnics and universities;

(d) better services and facilities, particularly the spread of rural water supply and sewerage schemes, clinics, health centres and hospitals;

(e) a changing range of job opportunity, following upon the contraction of employment in remote rural areas, and expansion in the towns, with a corresponding stimulus to population movements, and the demand for new industrial and residential building;

(f) more leisure, giving rise to demands in holiday areas for additional accommodation, and extra land for recreation, from playgrounds to country parks;

(g) earlier retirement and more elderly people, seen largely by planners as a special housing problem, particularly where retired people congregate in large numbers, as on the south coast.

In identifying the impact of these changes on the towns and villages of the rural regions, the mobility of the population seems to be particularly relevant. Mobility is an important element in social and economic change; two of its many facets are of direct concern to the country planner:

(1) the daily mobility of people going about their normal business, a movement which traces along roads, railways and other lines of physical communication, a pattern reflecting many aspects of social and economic life;[13]

(2) the change of residence of people moving from one locality or region to another, reflecting changes in employment, retirement and residence.

Both types of mobility appear to be increasing, and both have been the subject of studies by planners, geographers, and, in more recent years, mathematicians, who have applied techniques of mathematical model building to problems of population distribution and growth. There is evidence that a larger proportion of the population change residence quite frequently—in Norfolk the proportion is about 30 per cent in 5 years (mostly within the County)—and that a considerable number of people are involved in an increasing amount of journeying in their daily lives. Nevertheless, there has not been a sufficiently comprehensive survey to allow firm general conclusions to be drawn about daily or residential mobility in the rural regions. Instead, a picture has to be built up from a patchwork of urban land-use transportation,[14] and village, surveys. The picture obtained by this means tends to be selective in subject matter and statistically unsound, especially where comparisons are made. But it indicates the importance of mobility as a factor in planning in the rural regions, and the greater attention which must be paid to it in formulating planning policy in the future.

The rural regions contain a range of settlements, from the few large towns and cities, to the very large number of villages. Because the towns are the main centres of shopping, education, employment and entertainment, the town resident generally travels shorter distances, mainly within the town, while the village resident more frequently leaves the village, and travels much farther. The normal length of journey, to school, work, shops, entertainment, or in private visiting, in towns, in the rural regions, is seldom more than five miles, and is usually less than three. In contrast, travel out of the village to similar places normally involves journeys of more than three miles, and more often between six and ten miles. Some 90 per cent of journeys are wholly within town boundaries, while from many villages, even in remote rural districts, over half the population travel out of the village at least once a day. It is clear that the population in the rural regions is increasingly dependent on travel out of villages and hamlets (and some of the smaller towns) for much of its schooling, employment, shopping and leisure pursuits. With the generally poor frequency of public transport, the use of a car has become an essential part of the rural way of life.

In the towns in the rural regions, most children live within walking distance of school, and although some parents take their children to school by car, for safety as much as convenience, a large proportion walk to school, while others use public transport. Village children have been accustomed to travelling long distances to grammar school, but until fairly recently, a large proportion of children attended school in their own village. This situation is changing rapidly. Since the Education Act of 1944, the progressive reorganisation of primary and secondary education has meant more travelling, by more and younger children, to reach fewer but larger schools in the larger villages, and in the towns. Only the larger villages are likely to retain a junior (or middle level) school, and secondary education will normally be provided in the towns. Daily travel out of the village is likely to become a regular habit from the age of eight or nine.

As with school, so with work, an increasing proportion of country people travel out of their village daily, many to jobs in nearby towns. Whereas a large majority reside and work in the same town (e.g. 90 per cent in Norwich), between 25 and 75 per cent of villagers travel out of their village to work. The large variation in the village figure is due to differences in distance from urban centres of employment, differences in social class and income, and differences in the policy of the local planning authority towards speculative development. Generally, the nearer the town, the higher the proportion who work there. But the settlement of commuter population and speculative building have not been evenly distributed round towns, and a wide variation in local conditions is found. There is also a fairly marked contrast, between town and village, in the mode of travel to work. In Norwich, a large city by rural regional standards, nearly a fifth of the population walked to work (in 1967), a fifth cycled, a fifth travelled by public transport, and less than one-third travelled by car. In villages, the proportions are very different. On average, between one-tenth and one-twentieth use public transport; and where a large proportion work outside the village, up to 70 per cent may travel by car.

Apart from journeys to school and work, there is considerable travel to towns for shopping. In the past, this was mainly for luxury and specialised goods, but with supermarkets and discount stores flourishing in most centres, regular and frequent trips from village to town are becoming increasingly worthwhile. Unlike workers, shoppers make much greater use of public transport, partly because most shoppers are women, but also because the services offered to shoppers are more extensive than commuter services. Up to 60 per cent of journeys made by women out of their village are by bus (although note that this figure includes young women workers, who use bus services more than young men). Tastes in food and clothing and furniture have become more universal, raising both the quality and range of goods demanded by the country resident. The countryman, and woman, either travels to town to select from a wider range of goods, or makes good with a lesser choice locally.

Leisure facilities outside towns are mainly limited to what is provided by local clubs using village halls or schools. Comparisons are often made between the proportion of village residents who seek their leisure locally, and those who seek it further afield. The opportunity to travel to nearby towns makes a considerable difference, and comparisons between the support given to village and town pursuits have meaning only when related to age, marital status, numbers and ages of children, and transport facilities, characteristics sometimes ignored in assessments made by planners (and even by sociologists) of rural leisure. In the country, as well as in the town, television and radio compete with local entertainments, while the increasing ownership of cars gives more people the opportunity to participate in a wide range of sporting and other leisure activities. Young unmarried people, teenage and adult, obviously seek their entertainment outside the village to a greater extent than older, married people, with children, although in practice much depends on transport facilities and distance from town. A survey of Suffolk villages, by the sociology department of the University of East Anglia, showed that home-based leisure activities exceeded those outside the home by a large margin. Town and village activities were supported equally, and although people living nearer to the towns were attracted to them more often, it seems that the town complements what is provided in the village rather than competing with it.

Planners are giving increasing attention to the amount and length of daily movement in town and countryside, and are beginning to use fairly sophisticated methods of measuring and anticipating change. Mathematical formulae relating the location of homes, places of work, shopping centres, schools, places of entertainment, income and car ownership, have been developed and are being tested.[15] These mathematical 'models' give a 'theoretical' picture of daily mobility. How effective they will prove to be in practice has yet to be seen.

The daily movement out of a village is usually greater where there has been development on a scale sufficient to attract residents from nearby towns. A family which moves from town to a nearby village usually keeps strong links with the town, and members of the family travel regularly to the town for a variety of reasons. In this way, residential mobility stimulates a higher level of daily mobility, a characteristic considered so important by planners that they have made a broad division of the country into commuter—or pressure—areas, and remote—or non-pressure—areas. The boundary between the two represents the extent of urban influence on rural settlement growth (Map 6). In the bulletin *Settlement in the Countryside*, published in 1967 by the Ministry of Housing and Local Government,[16] a crude division is made between commuter areas within 15 miles of a town, and the remainder of the country, without any reference to the size of the town, or any attempt to justify the arbitrary figure of 15 miles. People seeking homes in villages and hamlets round towns will apparently travel considerable distances to work, but the pattern of commuter settlement depends on both the level of local demand, and the restraints imposed by local circumstance and planning policy.

The boundary between commuter and non-commuter areas is not a fixed line, but a transition between what is considered accessible and what is considered remote, between what has been selected for growth and what has not. There is evidence that over the past five to ten years, with continued increase in car ownership, and continued demand for homes in villages, the commuter areas have been extended, but whether this trend will continue is not at all certain. Much will depend on whether increasing ownership of cars is again reflected in a further demand to live outside the town, and whether this demand is accepted by planning authorities in their village policies. Very many planners seem to have already made up their minds against the development of villages to accommodate commuter population, sometimes on the grounds that it has a harmful effect on the social structure of the village, sometimes on the grounds that it is merely an extension of peripheral development round the town, a form of growth now much out of vogue. It is true that commuter growth has usually taken the form of new estates, large or small, added to a village or hamlet as a separate entity. This is often seen as a form of class segregation—a characteristic more normally associated with urban areas—and as an expression of the predominantly middle-class attitudes of the new residents. How far this is a legitimate reason to oppose the growth of a village near a town is a question requiring a more objective answer than most planners and planning authorities have yet given it.

In the Hampshire County Council's report on village life,[17] 'the preference for village life expressed by a substantial number of townspeople' was noted. This preference was 'leading to an increasing pressure for building in villages which cannot be met indefinitely without resulting in a change in the character of the village'. The report suggested that the pressure might be deflected back to the towns by 'creating an urban physical environment better than that found in some villages, but available at the same price'.

Whatever the reason people seek homes in smaller settlements away from towns, and whatever the form of development or the social class of the new residents, planners will find it difficult to sustain any policy aimed at limiting commuter growth in villages. It is significant that the Ministry of Housing and Local Government Bulletin on Settlement in the Countryside had little to say on the subject, and that few local planning authorities have a clear long-term policy on the size and pattern of commuter villages.

The movement of commuters into villages is only a part of a larger movement in the rural regions. A surprisingly large proportion of the population change residence each year, possibly up to 5 per cent. The village community is no longer one of people born and bred in the same village, or even in the country; but the idea that a large proportion of country people are 'local' dies hard. Nevertheless, studies carried out in various types of village, in various parts of the country, show that the proportion of adults born in their village of residence is seldom more than 40 per cent, and in many villages is much lower.[18] These studies suggest a steady movement of people into and out of most villages in the rural regions, possibly with a less mobile core of residents making up between one-third and one-half the population. Detail studies of this immobile group would be interesting to see whether it comprised any particular section of the community, or any particular income level or educational background.

Most published statistics on population movement are net figures summarising the result of much larger gross movements into and out of an area. These movements are distinguishable, but are not separately recorded. They comprise the movement from town to country of:

(1) families where the primary earner continues to work in the town—the so-called commuter growth;

(2) retired people, who select the more attractive areas, or those where property is relatively cheap, the sale of their house in town providing a welcome surplus of capital;

(3) other families or single persons, leaving urban employment for rural, a relatively small group.

From country to town of:

(4) families or single persons where the principal earner continues to work in the country—a relatively small-scale movement;

(5) families or single persons seeking both work and residence in the town—a larger movement comprising most of what is generally described as rural depopulation.

Within the countryside of:

(6) people changing jobs, or moving on retirement, together with their dependants;

(7) people getting married, or moving because of the death of a spouse, because of infirmity or for other social reasons.

Surveys have recorded the reasons why people move into villages, as to be nearer their place of work, to find better or cheaper housing, and to gain peace and quiet, covered three-quarters of the reasons given.[19] Less study has been made of the reasons why people leave the country for the town. The Scott Committee on Land Utilisation in Rural Areas (1941)[20] thought that people left mainly because of lack of facilities, but the reduction in the permanent labour force has probably been the more important reason.

A more comprehensive measure of the scale of these movements over, say, the past 5 to 10 years would help establish the quantity and content of change in the rural settlement pattern; studies in selected areas of the rural regions would give an indication of variations between one area and another, due to location, or different social and economic conditions.

Mobility has had some contradictory effects on rural life. It has allowed the townsman to become a country resident and it has made the country-man less dependent on the rural economy and on rural society. Migration has caused changes in class structure, particularly near the larger towns, and middle class, professional and the more affluent skilled workers have moved into the villages in sufficient numbers to have made a noticeable impact.[21]

There seems to be an increasing amount in common between newly-expanding suburbs and newly-expanding villages within the commuter zones. In both the suburbs and the commuter villages the residents expect shops, schools, places of recreation, public transport and street lighting to be provided but in neither does the provision usually come up to expecta-tion. From both suburb and village, people have to be willing to travel to a town centre to obtain many of the things they want, including some they think should be provided locally, but which are not. However, the suburb forms a physical part of the town, and as Professor John Rex pointed out in a paper to the 1968 Town and Country Planning Summer School, the suburbanist can choose to live within the confines of his or her suburb, or, more normally, can extend his social contacts to embrace people in the wider context of the whole town, an option also open to the villager but only with a much greater effort. Yet socially, where a family lives is probably of less significance than how they live, whether their house is privately owner-occupied or Council-rented, and whether the head of the household is a middle-class professional man, a skilled worker, or an unskilled labourer. The Hampshire report on village life found that

there is no typical pattern of village life in respect of the aspects investigated (work, shopping, spare-time activities, journeying and moving house); nor is there any marked difference between village life and town life. Instead, there are indications of distinctive groups in village society, each having its own way of life, attitudes and problems. These groups are probably largely based on age and level of income.

Ray Pahl and other sociologists have shown that the divisions of class are becoming more defined, both socially and spatially, by their location within a settlement, and they recognise definable styles of life, which probably have more affinity to class than to any other social factor.

It is significant that 'town' and 'country' do not rank as separate 'styles of life'. In the urbanised society of England and Wales, country life is no longer synonomous with farming, and there are few agricultural villages in the full sense of that term. Furthermore, townsmen and countrymen are now influenced by the same media of mass entertainment and the same forms of social and economic organisation. The cinema and radio, and more latterly, television, have been important influences leading towards similarity of attitude, and state regulated systems of education and welfare have tended to produce standard patterns of behaviour for many people. Country people today have the same labour-saving devices in the home, the same makes of car; they buy the same brands of canned and frozen foods, from the same types of supermarket and shops as their social counterparts in the towns. Their children attend the same types of school, take the same types of examination, marked by the same examiners, with the same standard of marking. It may be that new ideas still spread out from the towns to the country, and that fashions are common in the West End of London two years or more before they are seen in rural areas, but these time lags are not very significant in the time scale of the changes with which country planning is concerned.

With strong social and economic influences operating from outside the rural regions, and a weakening of the old economic and social structure from within, what form of social structure is likely to emerge in the rural regions? How far will the 'styles of life' recognised by sociologists in the conurbation regions be repeated in the rural? To what extent can the old country way of life survive the impact of the modern industrial urbanised society by which it is surrounded? However much the old hierarchy of squire, parson, gentleman farmer, tenant farmer and farm-worker may seem to remain, and however much the squire (or his ex-urban, ex-military, or retired successor) still thinks of himself as the squire, this old social structure has significance only in-so-far as local people want it to do so. In the past, when the landlord and the employer (often one and the same) had almost complete control of the villagers' economic well-being, and the parson had an equal measure of control over their spiritual life, the feudal hierarchy had a great deal of meaning. But with the real power passing to central and local government, to industry, commerce and the unions, and with a far greater degree of individual freedom of thought and action, the old social elite of the countryside is but a shadow of its former self, existing largely in its own reflection, and unable or unwilling to either wield its past power, or gracefully to pass away.

Nevertheless, it is still common for planners to try to measure the vitality of rural social life by the support given to the traditional local institutions, such as the Church, or the Women's Institute and similar clubs. Although in this way some measure of one aspect of country life can be gained, it gives only a narrow and incomplete view, and a largely false impression of social poverty. Professor Rex said at the 1968 Summer School . . . 'suburban man looks as socially and culturally impoverished as he does in the literature of romantic sociology and town planning simply because we have failed to look at his life as a whole' and his comment may be as applicable to the country planners' view of rural society as it is of the town planners' view of suburban society. As the village now seems to defy a clear-cut sociological definition, some planners are advocating a largely physical definition which embraces any settlement set within and physically dominated by the surrounding countryside. This might help overcome the emotive problem of defining town and village, but it leaves unanswered questions about the social structure and social networks in the rural regions and whether they differ significantly from the conurbations. The pattern of rural social life, of private and family connections and friendships, of personal and business and informal relationships needs to be measured as well as the more formal membership of clubs, if any index of the quality of rural life is to be obtained, relevant to the formulation of future policy in country planning.

3 Rural facilities and the village

Problem of provision [handwritten margin note]

Not so very many decades ago, the village was largely self-sufficient in that most villagers could obtain most of their requirements locally, even though many goods and services were brought in from urban and industrial areas. The inhabitants of hamlets and farms looked to the village for most of their needs, and what could not be obtained in the village was usually obtainable in the nearest market town. This high degree of self-sufficiency made the village the primary community in most rural regions. Widespread social and economic changes have combined to reduce the status of the village. Social life and trade have been stimulated in local market towns at the expense of the village, and in the regional centres at the expense of the towns and villages of the rural hinterland. The exact pattern of this change varies with each facility and service, with particular geographical and social circumstances, and, where local government services are concerned, with the policy of the local authority. Depopulation has raised doubts about the long-term viability of some major schemes of capital expenditure, such as new schools, and sewerage, while increasing car ownership has made difficulties in continuing to operate public transport services (i.e. increased personal mobility for the majority has led to less mobility for a minority). The rural population is now demanding a fairly high standard of shops, schools, health services, water supply and sewerage, at a time when these facilities are becoming increasingly expensive to provide and maintain in small places. There is a growing conflict between the expectation of each hamlet and village to be provided with a wide range of service and facility, and the organisation of those services and facilities into larger units of distribution. Some of the disparity between urban and rural living standards deplored by the Scott Committee's Inquiry into Land Utilisation in Rural Areas has gone, and what remains is mitigated to some extent by the greater ability to travel to town to obtain what is not provided locally. The rural population generally expects to find within fairly easy reach as much in the way of facilities as is provided in any suburb. In the *Analysis of the Survey of the Devonshire County Development Plan*,[22] it was suggested that a thriving rural community should possess the following:

(a) Public utilities—mains water, electricity and sewerage.

(b) Social facilities—primary school, places of worship, village hall and, possibly, a doctor's surgery.

(c) Shops, for day-to-day needs, and a post office.

(d) Employment, either in the village or conveniently situated nearby.

To this list might be added street lighting, recreation facilities, public transport and safe roads with good surfaces. It is a formidable list and one which, if accepted for every village of, say, 300 persons or more, would substantially increase the cost of supporting the rural population. The urban population already makes a large contribution to the provision of rural services,[23] and it may not be reasonable for the rural population to ask for more.

A few rural district councils are near to providing piped water and mains sewerage in every village and hamlet. But while piped water supplies have been extended to most settlements the great majority of rural district councils have made much less progress in providing sewerage facilities. The cost of sewerage in rural areas ranges from about £350 to £900 per house or other building connected, the variation in cost being due to a combination of topographical conditions—contouring and the disposition of properties—and design. The cost of providing sewerage is shared between Central and local government and between County and Rural District Councils, and only a part of the cost falls directly on the ratepayers of the rural district. In general terms the larger the village the lower the cost per connection and many rural district councils have tried to attract new development in the hope of justifying sewerage schemes where the cost is too high and where the lack of other facilities casts doubt on the wisdom of growth. *The Analysis of the Survey for the Devonshire County Development Plan* reports that

many improvements in, and extensions to, services and houses in rural areas have been undertaken in recent years in areas where the population is declining. There has been a tendency to build council houses, often in smaller groups, wherever there was an immediate demand, rather than concentrating them in a larger group in a village centrally and more conveniently placed. New sewerage schemes, which not only provide for existing development, but also tend to make provision for, and seek to attract, new development, have been undertaken in villages where new development is either inappropriate, or most unlikely, or both.

Advice is normally sought from local planning authorities on the likely growth of population in an area where sewerage facilities are being planned, but long-term advice usually errs on the high side, the estimates being used to ensure that design capacities are sufficient to meet foreseen —and some obviously unforeseen—circumstances: but they are not normally used to check the validity of schemes.

The education development plans of most county councils involved the building of a large number of secondary modern schools (to meet the needs of those not selected for grammar schools), the closure of many substandard primary schools and their replacement by fewer larger ones, either new or adapted from selected existing schools. The modern school building programme was largely achieved, but new primary school building was generally restricted to meeting additional demands from increasing population, estimates of population increase having been misleadingly low. Some schools have been closed, particularly in the more remote areas.[24] But the village school has survived twenty-four years of education planning under the Education Act, 1944, and the difficulties of educating children in very small schools remain. The policy of replacing the smaller village schools is still in operation, at least nominally.

The system of education outlined in the 1944 Education Act is being reviewed by most authorities. The Labour Government made it mandatory upon authorities to submit schemes for comprehensive secondary education, but the present Government has relaxed the mandatory requirement, leaving the choice between selection (for grammar and modern schooling) and the comprehensive system open to each authority. In the event, it seems as if most authorities are adopting some form of comprehensive education. Comprehensive secondary education generally means larger schools serving larger areas, and as mentioned in chapter two, secondary schools are likely to be retained only in the towns.[25]

The review of primary education could have a similar effect, but on a smaller scale. Most Education Authorities seem to favour a larger type of junior school, an intermediate level between the informality of infant education and the formality of the senior school. This larger type of junior school implies the greater separation of infants and juniors than is the present practice in rural areas, and either a new programme of junior school building in the larger villages and market towns, or the adaptation of secondary modern schools, where these are not retained as all-purpose secondary schools. With this system, many village schools are likely to be retained, but only as infant schools, for children between the ages of 4 or 5 and 7 or 8. Compared with the original education development plans of 1944, there may be more infants schools, but fewer and larger junior schools. Other authorities have adopted other primary school arrangements, but the general model is one of fewer schools in fewer places. It is uncertain how the relocation of schools will affect the location of new housing development, but Ray Pahl says of commuters that 'I am quite certain that one of the most crucial determinants of housing demand will be the future pattern of schools'. It seems logical that rural planning policy should aim at a high degree of correlation between housing and educational development, an aim not always achieved in present-day practice.

Hospital and specialist medical services are mainly located in regional and sub-regional centres, although some hospital boards inherited older buildings in the countryside which have been adapted to serve particular needs, such as geriatric units and the treatment of rheumatic diseases. The general practitioner remains the mainstay of local health services, supported by the district nurse, health visitor and pharmacist (or where there is no chemist, by the doctor's own dispenser). In a paper prepared for a conference of rural research workers,[26] by J. B. Ayton and the author, an assessment was included of the population needed to support local health services. 'One doctor may have 2,000–2,500 patients, but a three-doctor practice, now usual in rural areas, requires at least 6,000 people to support it. The standards recommended by the Ministry of Health for health visitors, midwives, and home nurses, advocate between 5,000 people (for the nurse) and 8,000 people (for the health visitor).'

Unlike the education and health services, the pattern of shops cannot be affected so directly by Government or Local Government policy, and shopping tends to reflect more accurately the expression of choice by many individuals, where they go and what they buy. Shops are the last link in a chain from grower or manufacturer to consumer, and changes in methods of wholesale distribution and in consumer demand may profoundly affect both the number and disposition of shops; for example, large-scale organisation and greater consumer demand and private transport, have given the supermarket an advantage over the independent grocer. Shops in many villages have closed and others may be expected to close in the future. In many villages there are now no shops, although the travelling shop does a little to fill the gap. In many large villages,

c

which once had thriving centres, the only shops likely to survive are general stores. The small country town is expanding its shopping facilities, usually in the provision of larger shops, rather than more shops, and the additional facilities usually include at least one supermarket. The larger country towns and regional centres are gaining in trade, relatively at the expense of the small town and actually at the expense of the village. The extent to which these changes will influence the distribution of population and development is uncertain, but it seems clear that only market towns and very large villages will continue to offer anything approaching a reasonable range of local shops for those who wish to be within walking distance of local facilities.

A Cambridgeshire County Council survey[27] shows that the facilities in villages improve with size: villages of 170–600 persons having a pub, post office, hall and general store; villages of 600–1,100 persons having also a primary school, playing field and garage; villages of 1,100–1,800 persons having also a police house or station, butcher, ladies' hairdresser and doctor; villages of 1,800–3,000 persons having also an electrical goods shop, licensed club, hardware store and gentlemen's hairdresser; and villages of more than 3,000 persons having also a secondary school and chemist.

Studies carried out in Norfolk suggest that, with the present size and distribution of villages, local facilities might be maintained at a level of

one district nurse or health visitor for each 4–5 villages,
one group surgery for each 6–7 villages,
one junior school to serve each 6–10 villages,
and a reasonable range of shopping facility in only 1 in 10 villages.

The Norfolk studies also showed that the minimum population needed to support local rural facilities is about 5,000 persons.[28] Whether this population should be accommodated in one large settlement or in a number of small ones is a subject of considerable debate, but it is a question which the rural population will have to decide as the process of rationalisation continues to deprive people in smaller villages of their local facilities. It is also a question about which planning, education and health authorities will have to decide their policies—whether to locate facilities in one centrally located place and guide residential development into that place. It is a question which raises strong emotions, and where the local planning authority adopts a central place or key village policy, cries of 'our dying villages' and 'the planners are killing rural life' are heard and attention is focussed, yet again, at that hardy annual, the rural planning conference, on the minimum size for a viable rural community. There have been many suggestions about the population level below which village life is supposed to become too limited, but few of these suggestions have been based either on an objective sociological study or on any clear indication of what is meant by the term viable when applied to a rural community. In most cases a 'viable' community has been taken to mean one where the population is sufficient to support both local facilities and local social activities, and estimates of size have varied from 500 to 8,000. In *The English Village*, Penguin 1952, V. Bonham Carter suggested that 'villages of less than 500 persons are not usually able to afford the upkeep of all the services, amenities and institutions that give a place a strength and a character of its own'. In a discussion group of town planners, led by Andrew Thorburn,[29] 'the suggestion was made that the optimum size for a village was 8,000, but most members thought that the alternative bid of 800 put forward by a representative from a Welsh county was more reasonable'. It may be that discussions about the optimum size of villages are of mainly academic interest, but they are viewed with scepticism and misgiving by many country people. If ever consulted, they would prob-ably support R. W. Stirling,[30] who said, in a paper on rural development in 1953, that, so far as the best size of village is concerned, 'we none of us can be dogmatic on the subject but opinions have been expressed that whilst a minimum of about 700 should be aimed at—largely from the standpoint of satisfactory primary school provision—beyond a figure of 1,500 a village becomes socially "difficult" '. The same upper limit was quoted in a more recent definition of a village in a report by the West Suffolk County Council on Rural Planning (1968).[31]

There is a clear conflict between the impressions people hold about the ideal size of village, and the population needed to support village schools, shops, medical practices, and transport and other services. The figure of 5,000 suggested in the Norfolk studies is met with sheer disbelief by most rural communities.

Most country people think of a settlement of 5,000 inhabitants as a small town and many well-established country towns are smaller than this. Quoting again from the West Suffolk report, 'The older definition of a village as being a closely integrated community is not wholly accept-able today when the range of size and function of each village is so variable and subject to change'; it may be that the village as a social centre has no future, and that the rural regions will contain only small towns or hamlets. The term village no longer has any precise social and economic meaning, and is now used loosely to describe country settlements which are not towns. There is a wide range of settlement in the rural regions and, to avoid confusion and ambiguity in these commonly used terms, hamlet, village and country town need to be defined.

A *hamlet* ranges from a small group of houses, possibly including farmhouses, to a settlement large enough to support a shop or shops, public house, filling station, infant school and services and facilities at that level.

A *village* supports a fairly wide range of local shops, infant and junior schools, possibly a repair garage and services at that level. The village normally serves a number of hamlets, particularly for shopping and education, but also for religious services.

The *country town* differs from the village by virtue of the scale of the services it provides. It usually contains secondary modern and grammar schools, a factory or two, a concentrated shopping centre with a fairly wide range of shops serving more than local needs, and a range of services and facilities such as youth clubs and old people's homes. The country town ranges considerably in size and function from the minor commercial and employment centre of 5,000 to 15,000 population to the major commercial, industrial, administrative and communications centre of 30,000 population or more. A large part of the employment in rural regions is concentrated in the larger country towns.

The terms hamlet, village and country town are thus given functional meanings related to the services they provide, rather than to their social character or population. By this definition, the great majority of rural settlements are—or will become—hamlets, and there will be few real villages.

4 Employment and industry and the small country town

The growth of population, and new development round the larger towns and cities—and the conflict this raises with the preservation of the country-side—has dominated planning thinking in the rural regions since 1947. This was a logical consequence of the attention given to the subject of urban sprawl by the Committee on Land Utilisation in Rural Areas (Scott Committee, 1941). Yet the most important and far-reaching changes in the rural regions have arisen not from pressures from outside, but by change from within. Throughout the rural regions a continuous decrease in the number of men employed full time in agriculture, coupled with a decline in local ancillary trades such as the blacksmith, has completely changed the economic and social structure. In some areas the decrease in the number of agricultural workers has been over 4 per cent per annum, and it is expected by agricultural economists that the decrease will continue for some years yet. Forecasts vary, but a government study suggests that the number of regular full-time male agricultural workers in 1981 might be only half what it was in 1966.[32] The rate of decline varies with the type of farming, the size and organisation of holdings, Government and Union policy, the attitude of the farmer and the rate of capital investment in farming, but the general trend is a persistent decline in the labour force.

An interesting illustration of how farming is changing is afforded in the Great Yarmouth and Lowestoft area. The development of the frozen food industry in those towns has meant that large acreages have been devoted to peas, beans and other vegetables on farms within reasonable transporting distance. The regular labour force on many farms has already been reduced to below the level predicted for 1981. Those who remain are employed mainly on cultivation and routine maintenance work. Where grain and grass are grown as a crop local labour harvests them, but the vegetable crops are usually harvested by contract labour, mostly employed by the freezers, who may also arrange the sowing of the crop. The organisation is on a large scale, and a common sight, at harvest time, is a field with fifteen to twenty machines, pea viners, tractors, trucks and trailers, working to a tight schedule, by which the fresh vegetables are delivered to the factory, and frozen, within two hours of harvesting. If this gives a foretaste of general agricultural organisation in high productivity areas, it suggests that a considerable part of the labour force may be brought out to the farms on contract, from the nearby towns. With other seasonal labour demands at other times of the year, in sugar refineries, using local beet, in fruit freezing and canning, and in the holiday industry, a mobile and adaptable labour force may be characteristic of the future.

Unlike many other industries, reduction in the agricultural labour force does not normally result in redundancy, the reduction in numbers being effected through lower recruitment rather than by the discharge of established and experienced workers, But the long-term effect is much the same; each year a few more school-leavers find difficulty in securing work locally and have to look further afield. A study of the Fakenham Employment Area, made by the Norfolk County Planning Department,[33] showed a persistent movement of young people out of this largely agricultural area. The movement was closely related to declining employment opportunity, and if employment prospects were not dramatically improved, migration out of the area would continue apace. Rationalisation in the agricultural industry has also meant fewer farms—the trend towards larger holdings and the amalgamation of smaller ones has meant fewer farmers as well as farmworkers. The number of people directly involved in agriculture or in some way dependent upon it has been so much reduced that agriculture no longer supports the majority of the rural population.

Agriculture still provides a very large part of the gross annual income of the rural regions, and makes a substantial contribution to their prosperity, but the farmer uses much of his income outside the local community, from which he is becoming increasingly independent. He and his family tend to use the nearby towns as much as the nearby villages, and he is no longer a major employer of local labour. Even in the more remote areas, a relatively small proportion of the population now enters the agricultural industry, whether as farmers, farmworkers or trainees. A larger proportion seek work in other occupations, sometimes travelling daily out of their home areas, sometimes moving residence to their new place of employment; where the latter have not been replaced by a compensating inward movement of population, there has been net depopulation; where local natural increase in population has not matched the depopulation, there has been an actual population decline.

Two changes are characteristic of almost the whole of the rural regions —a decreasing personal involvement in agriculture, and a natural increase in population (by the excess of births over deaths)—and these changes apply to both areas of population growth and to areas of population decline. What distinguishes growth areas from decline areas in the rural regions is the ability of the growth areas to attract new forms of employment, or sufficient numbers of commuters and retired people to compensate the decline in agricultural employment. A substantial part of the rural regions has a static or declining population. Many authorities, faced with a relatively high birth-rate and a paucity of employment opportunity, have supported local campaigns, to attract new industrial development. The degree of support given to these campaigns has varied from purely technical advice to the acquisition of land, and the development of trading estates, complete with roads and sewers, and the campaigns have had a varying degree of success.

The most successful have been those associated with the Town Development Act, and a view, today, of the thriving industrial town of Thetford, compared with the depressed village it was not much more than ten years ago, illustrates the effectiveness of town development as a means of attracting industry and population into small towns in rural regions. But, most of the industrial development campaigns have been operated outside the scope of the Town Development Act, to provide employment for the existing population, rather than to expand by introducing both new industry and population. The industrial development campaigns have shown that it has proved easier to attract industry to the larger than the smaller towns, that little industry has been attracted to the villages, and that much of the new industry which has been established in small towns has been female-employing, whereas most of the jobs 'lost' in agriculture in the surrounding areas have been male. There has been little published about the type and location of new industry established in the rural regions, but there has been much discussion of the validity, and practicability, of introducing industry into rural locations. Rural industrial development has been the subject of regular papers and discussions at Town and Country Planning Summer Schools. In 1953, R. L. Stirling reported that at County and District level, a policy is being followed of doing everything possible to attract industry to many market towns. But in the main, it is only

succeeding to the extent of attracting industry sufficient to absorb a concealed
reserve of labour.

In 1957, in a paper on the planning problems of rural areas, Geoffrey
Clark took the view that

this process of rural industrialisation should be allowed to proceed naturally
and steadily, rather than that we should entice industrial units away from their
normal settings and in doing so create pockets of urbanity where they should
not be. The real point . . . is that the major area of farming England has to put
its own house in order and rely, in general, on its own agricultural industry
for long-term prosperity,

a prospect which implies a considerable rate of rural depopulation from
many areas. However, at the 1964 Summer School, Professor Wibberley
took a somewhat less pessimistic view, and, in a paper on the Changing
Rural Economy of Britain, he said:

Industrial employment is more economic in the countryside than it was because
of the mobility and lower relative costs of moving power, raw materials, people
and products. Even so, the larger enterprises will favour the rural edges of
thriving conurbations (and thus be outside the rural regions as defined in this
book) and the larger country towns possessing major road access. The remote
villages and small country towns are of little attraction to most industries as
possible locations of new factories or branch plants. Some of them can, however, be tied in with new job opportunities under a system of wise regional
development which takes account of hierarchies or constellations of settlement,
and the fact that rural Britain now operates on a highly intricate system of
rural commuting.

W. F. Luttrell, in a paper to the same Summer School, recognised four
levels of industrial organisation, which could be related to their locational
requirements:

(1) The new main works: this is the plant which has become the firm's
centre for the range of goods or product division in question. . . .
(2) The self-contained full-scale plant: this has the full array of management
and organisational services on the spot. Generally it makes some of the firm's
products completely, without the need for them to be sent to another of its
plants. In size, it may be in the 250–500 employment range, but may be much
larger, at a thousand or more. . . .
(3) The intermediate branch: this may employ one or two hundred workers,

which is large enough to justify quite considerable organisation and management on the spot, but is not treated as completely self-contained.

(4) The small subsidiary branch: this is usually the offshoot or duplication of only one department of a factory, looked after by someone of little more than foreman status, and completely controlled from its parent factory which would provide its work programme, accounts and most other services. It would typically employ 40 or 50 people, often female; some go up to 100, but if they have more they warrant more elaborate organisation on the spot.

Mr Luttrell went on to say:

Small or medium sized subsidiary branches can be operated quite successfully within a radius of about 30 miles from their parent plant. Therefore, where there is an industrial centre which provides the right conditions for a 'main works' to grow, one of its methods of expansion may be by throwing out off-shoots to smaller towns within this radius. The smallest branches may even go to villages; but for a number of reasons the country town with a population of, say, 5,000 upwards is found to provide a better base than a village [for the self-contained full-scale plant]. A smallish rather isolated town . . . will not be very suitable even though the total number of people available is adequate [as] it has been found that a plant of this sort does better if it is in or very near to the main industrial complex. . . .

In this context, it will be interesting to see how the mid-Wales Newtown Development Corporation progresses in its attempt to expand Newtown, a small rural centre of about five and a half thousand people.

The introduction of new industry into small country towns has succeeded in widening local employment opportunities but more for women than for men, and, taking the small country town and its village hinterland together, the job opportunities for men are probably fewer than they were some years ago, but more than they would have been but for the industrial development policies of local authorities.

At the end of the second World War, the country town seemed to have a secure future (Professor Wibberley even referred to it as the basis for future regional planning). In the rural regions, this promise has not been fulfilled. Although the country town has gained trade from the surrounding villages, and has become the main local centre, it has lost both trade and functions to the larger towns and cities. As long ago as 1953, R. L. Stirling pointed out that 'many country towns—once focal points in the social and economic life of the countryside—now struggle along with diminished trade, meagre rate revenues, and facilities which

no longer fully satisfy the needs of countryfolk'. Even so, country towns
continue to play an important role in country life and one of the characteristics which most surprises the visitor is the wide range of service
and facility offered even in towns of less than 10,000 population. There
are country towns of between 3,000 and 10,000 population, with a range
of shops which may include a first-class grocer, a chemist, a small department store and even a branch of Woolworth's, in addition to the usual
food and provision merchants. There is usually a general post office and
branch offices of most of the national banking companies. Sales and service
are offered for most makes of British car, and, possibly, for some makes
of foreign car, as well as for agricultural machinery. There is usually a
public hall, sometimes a cinema, and, more rarely, a swimming pool.
In these towns the education authority usually concentrates its secondary
school facilities. Local medical practices are usually centred on it and it
carries other professional services, including solicitors, accountants, architects and surveyors, auctioneers and estate agents. The reason for this
wide range is to be found in the extent to which people in the surrounding
villages, hamlets and farms use the country town, extending its service
area and bringing the population supporting it up to a figure usually
between 20,000 and 30,000 (see diagram).

The population of most small country towns has increased in the past
decade or two, and in many there has been a small inward migration to
add to a natural increase. But in the more remote country areas, the
population in the parishes surrounding the towns has decreased, with the
result that the future of these towns as service centres is in some doubt.
With the trend towards larger units of distribution and administration,
larger support populations are needed merely for the town to remain as
it is. In remote areas, country towns which do not seek and obtain new
employment and additional population are likely to lose at least some part
of their service functions. In less remote parts of rural regions, both the
town and surrounding area may be gaining population, and—depending
on local planning policies—may continue to do so. But nearness to a large
town or city, which is usually a stimulus for population and employment
growth, may also become a problem. The small town can seldom compete effectively against the large town, with its cut-price supermarkets,
multiple traders and other concerns of national standing. The future of
few small country towns is assured, though few are in any very immediate
peril; decline, if it comes, is likely to be insidious and, for that reason, all

the more dangerous. With a strong professional and trading middle class which controls the main institutions of the town, the complacency of most small town communities is surprising. Observation suggests that a high proportion of the present tradesmen, councillors, and partners of professional practices are near to retirement. It may be that they do not see their sons and daughters following in their footsteps, but the community as a whole may live to regret their apparent lack of concern.

5 Communications

National and regional lines of communication generally link the major towns and industrial areas and form part of what is popularly called the economic infrastructure of the conurbations. Major roads and railways pass through rather than to the rural regions, and it is only the lesser roads and railways which reflect the economic structure and settlement pattern of rural areas. The same two levels apply to the measure of accessibility, the higher reflecting the time and distance from the conurban centres, the lower taking the same measure from centres within the rural regions. The motorways in the rural regions have been imposed to serve the adjoining conurbations (Map 7). Nevertheless, the presence of motorways and inter-conurban trunk roads is having a considerable effect on the pattern of growth in the rural regions, just as the railways had in the last century. The report of the discussions on 'Living and Working in the Countryside', prepared as part of the second Countryside in 1970 conference included a reference to the probable effect of new and improved roads:

In lowland areas . . . one major factor affecting natural growth is the distance which can be covered in about an hour . . . the development of motorways, dual carriageways and rural roads will have the general effect of increasing the distance that can be travelled in this time. The physical distance between residence and centres of employment, services, shopping and entertainment may therefore be expected to increase as time-distance decreases. Major service centres may become fewer in number as the distances increase. New major and minor centres are likely to develop close to the new lines of road communication. Towns and villages more remote from the main arteries may stagnate or decline, resulting in the need for a system of priorities of capital expenditure on rural roads.

Peter Hall[34] has suggested that there has been a boom in motorway building, which is now coming to an end. But he says that it is too early to measure the impact of the motorways.

It will take some years for the point to come generally home that motorways effectively double or treble possible commuting distances . . . but no one should doubt that by the 1980's, the sure result will be unprecedented pressure on what are now, still, rural retreats. Like the railways a century or more ago, the motorways will revolutionise our social lives.[35]

Furthermore, according to the report 'Living and Working in the Countryside', the 'shape of existing settlements may well be changed if they are appropriately located with respect to the new communication links . . . clusters of new houses with associated local services are likely to appear adjacent to the new roads but not on them'.[36]

A great many country roads are merely old farm tracks and local rights of way 'made up' with a layer of tarmac. They are generally narrow, poorly aligned and without footpaths; the traffic flows are light but tend to be faster than the conditions of the road warrants, but possibly slower than the distances to be covered necessitate. Pedestrians and cyclists, particularly young children walking or riding to school, are at risk, probably at greater personal risk than in some urban areas. There are many thousands of miles of sub-standard rural roads and the resources available for their improvement are strictly limited. Improvement is likely only where the country road forms part of a wider network associated with urban and industrial development, or large-scale holiday traffic movement. The lack of funds may save the charm of many country lanes and village streets, but only at the cost of their remaining a hazard. The country road pattern bears little relation to the needs of a highly mobile rural population, and there has been little attempt to rationalise the system beyond the classification and improvement of the inter-urban (and mainly inter-conurban) routes. The recent definition of roads into Strategy and other classified roads by the Ministry of Transport seems a particularly urban concept which largely ignores rural needs. However, some county highway authorities have defined a country road system and road improvements, and to a less degree road maintenance, are being restricted to this system. The selection of these country roads tends to reflect existing conditions rather than any trend or policy for future rural settlement. Instead, a plan for country roads linking country towns, villages and hamlets to major roads is needed, with separate roads linking the smaller villages and hamlets only where a major road is not conveniently placed.

It is a strange anomaly that whereas lack of funds has prevented the improvement of many country roads, where funds have been made available, they have not always been used to the greatest advantage.

Although major road schemes have to be justified on traffic grounds before they can attract a grant, there is doubt about the viability of some schemes which have been carried out. This is not to suggest excessive cost in engineering terms—costs which are normally lower in rural areas in any event—but more adequate means should be employed to ensure a reasonable return from the capital outlay. Furthermore, priorities seem to be based on local knowledge and local opinion (rather than any more objective assessment). The selection of roads to form the basic country road structure (the possibility of new roads being built to serve the rural population is extremely remote) should follow a cost benefit appraisal, whereby the cost of maintenance and minimum necessary improvement per mile per local resident served should be set against some defined cost standards, just as rural sewerage schemes are expected to cost no more than a standard figure per connection set by the Ministry of Housing and Local Government. The country road cost standard would be adjusted to take account of regional variations in population density and settlement pattern.

A made-up road extends into nearly every village and hamlet; in the quite recent past branch railway lines also extended deep into rural areas but the rail closures in the past 10 to 15 years have left the roads dominant, and large country areas rely exclusively on road transport. The countryman has not been slow to take advantage of the car and car ownership is generally higher per head of population in rural areas than urban. One of the reasons for high car ownership figures—and partly also the result of them—is that rural public transport services are poor, and are deteriorating, a circumstance which must be as worrying to the transport operators as it is for those who continue to reside in the country (especially those who, for reasons of age, infirmity, finance, or, more simply, choice, do not have the regular use of private transport). Although the high rate of car ownership may be a measure of the inadequacy of rural public transport, it also shows the extent to which many country families have gone in order to extend the range of facility, service, opportunity and social life beyond the previously limited confines of the village, and those few places which can be reached by public transport regularly and frequently. The motor vehicle has given the countryman the opportunity to widen his social life and his horizons and it can only be good that he is doing so. The planner has thought of the car mainly in terms of the associated urban problems of congestion, but the motor vehicle has become an important adjunct to country life, and one which will continue to have a profound influence on the way people live and where they live. The report 'Living and Working in the Countryside' suggested that '. . . possession of private transport is likely to give the farmer, or farm labourer, a more open choice between living on the land, and living in some more nucleated settlement'.[37] The car, the travelling shop, the school bus (taking children to use facilities in schools in nearby towns, as well as collecting from home and returning children from the local school), the private coach outing, and the regular bus service, all reduce the social and economic isolation of the rural settlement.

Country public transport services are oriented mainly towards towns and cities, and do not give much opportunity for travel between villages, unless they lie on inter-urban routes. The most economic rural services seem to be those designed to carry school children, commuters (mainly young working women, since the majority of men travel to work in private transport) and shoppers on market days. There are also services related to entertainment and other facilities in the major towns, but these services are often considered to be particularly inadequate. The demand for public transport services is difficult to assess, as information about the use made of existing facilities is extremely limited, but some idea who uses buses and trains to and from some of the main regional and sub-regional centres is being gleaned from transportation surveys. Current use, however, gives an incomplete measure of demand, because the use of public transport is restricted by its own inadequacy, by the slowness and infrequency of most services, its discomfort, and the limited range of need for which it provides.

Although the Licensing Authorities and Operators take account of public need, they cannot hold up the retraction of services, in the face of increasing use of private transport by increasing numbers of people. Throughout the countryside, in the rural regions, the present situation is becoming increasingly unsatisfactory, and in places seems to touch on the absurd. Where railway passenger services are withdrawn, the provision of alternative bus services has been a condition of closure, the bus service being subsidised at a cost less than the operating loss on the railway. Thus for a time, bus services in the area improve and reach a standard higher than yet achieved elsewhere.

The *White Paper on Transport and Traffic*, published in 1967,[38] pointed to the need to maintain rural transport services, and the Transport Act,

1968, makes provision for services to be subsidised by local government. At present, British Rail deficits are met by the Government, and this acts as a form of subsidy, but it has not saved many branch lines, as the railways intend to close non-profitable lines unless selected for retention on social need grounds. Bus companies operate many rural services at the expense of the more profitable urban services, but in the rural regions the operation of all local public transport services seems far from assured, and subsidies to bus operators may be necessary. But it is doubtful whether the operators should be subsidised for running half empty double-decker buses, the basic design for which was developed in 1933 for use in large conurbations, at a time when a motor-car was still a luxury. It has been advocated by students of rural transport that the various rural services should be combined; a multi-purpose vehicle could be developed, capable of carrying people to country towns for a variety of purposes (attending school, hospital, shopping or visiting) and carrying parcels and mail to local distribution centres. These multi-purpose services would be operated by a bus company, or, in default of a willing operator, by the local authority, in partnership with the postal and health authorities.

A cost benefit (or appraisal) technique, similar to that suggested for the country road programme, could be applied to the operation and subsidy of rural public transport. Transport subsidies will have to compete for relatively scarce financial resources with other services provided by the local authorities, and the value of subsidising any route will have to be judged alongside other possibilities for serving the area. The cost of the service per head of the population per mile could act as a cost yardstick, to be used for comparison with some standard figure laid down by the Ministry of Transport for the guidance of local authorities.

Adapting and, where necessary, subsidising transport services is one approach to the challenge to public transport from increasing car ownership and the generally scattered settlement pattern in the rural regions. Another, rather longer term, approach is to effect a change in the settlement pattern, by guiding development into a more concentrated form, with fewer, larger settlements where transport facilities can be most easily supported, and where they might even become self-supporting.

The shape, distribution and size of settlements had been much influenced by transport and lines of communication. To quote one very familiar example, the development of commuter villages falls into three distinct phases, the first related to the railway, the second to road public transport and the third to private road transport. In the first two periods, from about 1890 to about 1950, commuter village development tended to follow railway and bus timetables, and routes. Since the motor-car has become the primary means of rural transportation, commuter development has become more widespread (in spite of the stricter planning control operative since the 1950's), although the primary road network seems to have influenced developers and local authorities in deciding the direction and scale of development round the larger towns and cities. People faced with the prospect of a daily journey to and from the town to work seem generally unwilling to live too far from a main road or public transport route. Where the road system is radial from the town, growth areas tend to resemble the circle by which they are represented in the Ministry of Housing and Local Government's Bulletin on *Settlement in the Countryside*,[39] but more in the form of a star with rounded-off points.

6 Settlement structure and policy

The extent to which the pattern of settlement—through the location and size of towns and villages—influences the provision and maintenance of services in rural areas, and the degree of convenience in rural life, does not seem to have been fully appreciated, even by town and country planners. The concern of most planners seems to be with conservation, and with the siting and design of buildings in villages and hamlets, largely to the exclusion of the wider issues of settlement size and distribution. Regional and sub-regional planning, even in the rural regions, is seen generally as involving the pattern of urban settlement, rural areas providing the back-cloth against which urban problems are resolved. For example, the green belts and the restrictive policy they embody are wholly oriented towards the towns and the cities the green belts surround, and they have little to do with living conditions in the area they 'sterilise', and thereby protect from urban encroachment. The definition of the Country Areas suggested by Hampshire County Council[40] as a means whereby predominantly agricultural areas are protected against urban pressures, seems to do little more than apply a weaker green belt policy on a wider scale.

From the discussion of the social and economic background to country planning in the previous chapters, it is clear that the situation in the rural regions is changing radically. 'Yet in our rural development policy we tend to cling to the old pattern of settlement, even though the mobility of goods and services and of people have changed almost out of all recognition to what it was when these settlements were in their heyday.'[41] The policies of most local planning authorities seem to be directed towards maintaining a form of status quo in the rural regions, by assuming a continuation of present trends in population growth and housing. The rate and distribution of growth are not normally questioned. Neither the booklet *New Houses in the Country*, published in 1960,[42] nor the later Bulletin on *Settlement in the Countryside*, gave much advice on the spatial or size distribution of villages and hamlets, or whether the existing pattern could be sustained economically, or socially, in the future. The booklet was mainly concerned with the prevention of sporadic building in the

open countryside, and the Bulletin mainly with the techniques available
for planning individual settlements. Nevertheless, the Bulletin gave passing attention to settlement policy in relation to the development plan,
and suggested that the plan should include:

(a) an approximate estimate of the future population planned for in
rural settlements, broken down to show the implications of policies of
restriction or expansion applying to groups of villages; and,

(b) lists of settlements to be expanded substantially or tightly restricted,
with a statement of the criteria on which the decisions are based.

Some of the more forward looking county planning authorities in the
rural regions have adopted policies aimed at encouraging a limited number
of towns and villages to grow while leaving the majority of villages to
remain static or decline. A good example of the thinking underlying this
policy of selective development is given in a series of reports on rural
Nottinghamshire, prepared by the County Director of Planning.[43] In
the report on the rural district of East Retford, published July 1966, the
view is expressed that increasing demands are likely to be experienced in
the rural district for residential accommodation.

Of the methods of accommodating population growth in a rural district of the
character of East Retford it is considered preferable to expand a limited number
of communities carefully selected, rather than to attempt to spread development
somewhat evenly over a large number of villages. In this way the new growth
will be concentrated so as to permit the provision of schools and public services
on an economic basis, and to ensure that the selected communities are conveniently located to employment. This means generally altering the character
of the selected villages, possibly even drastically, so it seems highly desirable
that villages which have special attraction, visual or historical, should not be
chosen as expansion or growth villages.

The report advocated the selection of 6 out of 54 parishes where plans
would be prepared for major growth, to accommodate 8,500 people out
of a total of 13,500 population increase anticipated in the rural district 'in
the future' (Map 12). By this policy, the population living in the towns,
and in the villages selected for expansion, would be increased, and the
problem of servicing the smaller rural communities would be reduced in
scale—though not necessarily made any easier.

There is comparatively little capital available for development in the
rural regions and the scope for planned change is not great. Economic
conditions vary between and within the rural regions. Increases in

employment are mainly centred in the towns, and population growth is likely to be also centred there and in the surrounding villages. The 'commuter areas' round the larger towns and cities in the rural regions are being extended, and the remote areas are being diminished, as the demand for accommodation in the villages, and the 'acceptable' commuting distance, increase. Population trends differ considerably, and the potential for change also varies significantly. The report 'Living and Working in the Countryside', prepared for the Countryside in 1970 conference, linked the future structure and function of rural settlement with urban and industrial pressures, suggesting that

the pattern of rural settlement in the future will be influenced by history, population increase, increased mobility and planning decisions. Population pressure will require more 'new towns' and 'expanded towns'. . . . The functions and character of rural settlements are likely to change as population and industry are further dispersed from the metropolitan centres. The life of village and country town is no longer dominated by agriculture, and different types of rural settlements, appropriate to other occupations, must be expected in the future; settlements characterised by commuting; settlements relying on seasonal demands from a town population which increasingly spends its leisure time in the countryside and at the coast; and settlements changed by the economic, demographic, and social consequences of industrial dispersal.

Where population growth is likely to be fairly considerable, it should be relatively easy to stimulate expansion in the selected centres, and the more difficult problem might be found in restricting it in the rest. Even with some minimum population in mind for each selected centre, there will be a range of choice between individual settlements, and between the general level of concentration or dispersal—into the country towns and larger villages only or into a wider range of village—and this choice is likely to be the greatest round the larger towns and cities in the rural regions. A study of various forms of development round Norwich, with more or less dispersal of population, is being made by the University of East Anglia, and should give planning authorities some guidance on the relative costs and benefits of concentrating growth or dispersing it.

Where population trends or planning policies suggest that a lower rate of growth may be expected, a policy of selective development of larger settlements is only likely to be achieved by influencing the direction of local migration, by persuading people who are moving house that they

will find a better life in the selected larger settlements, by making it easier
to find homes and jobs, and by providing higher standards of shopping,
transport and schooling. In these areas of low growth potential, the
success of the policy will also be dependent on persuading local people
of the merit of not attempting the expansion of too many centres, possibly
of restricting growth to the towns and the largest villages only. R. L.
Stirling, in a paper to the 1953 Town and Country Planning Summer
School, pointed out that 'any plan for the countryside which is based on
a gradual redistribution of the present population and a definite programme of development whereby some villages get much needed services
in advance of others, will always be subject to . . . the strength and influence of parochial and sectional representations'. Most parish councils
express a hope for some measure of growth in their village, and this
hope is normally reflected in some degree by Rural District Councils and
County Planning Committees. In the words of Andrew Thorburn, 'there
is a tradition in this country that every existing settlement, large or small,
has the right to grow in size'.[44] Planning policy in rural regions is very
much concerned with denying that deeply felt 'right'. While planners
see the need to select centres for the comprehensive development of
housing, services and facilities, local people often see the selective development of some settlements very much at the expense of the others, where
'non-growth' is interpreted as a step towards the ultimate death of the
village. There is little doubt that villages and hamlets not selected for
expansion will suffer a relative if not actual decline in population and will
move down the hierarchial scale of social and economic status.

In advocating any policy of selective growth, not only the reason for
the policy will need to be made clear, but also the basis for the selection
of particular towns and villages will have to be clearly stated if the policy
is to be generally accepted. Where Local Planning Authorities have
adopted this type of policy for rural development, selection of development centres or key towns and villages has usually been based on the
capital value and spare capacity of public services and social facilities,
particularly of schools and sewerage. Sporadic building in the countryside
was countered by allowing building in the gaps in the villages in what
became known as infilling; selection between villages based on the spare
capacity of services might well be described as economic infilling, having
the merit of ensuring full use of committed public expenditure. However,
as a basis for determining the long-term, future pattern of settlement, it

seems too limited and some other, broader, basis of selection needs to be developed.

There are considerable capital assets in towns, villages and hamlets, in the form of housing of adequate standard, schools, water mains and the electricity distribution system, roads, village and town halls and recreation grounds. Selection implies some wastage of these assets at an accelerated rate, and the cost of this needs to be balanced against the benefits of a less dispersed population distribution. A technique of cost-benefit analysis needs to be developed by which various patterns of development can be tested[45] to see which gives the maximum advantage in reducing costs of distribution and transportation, the least wastage of existing assets and the greatest social benefit (in so far as the latter is capable of being measured in these terms). Research is needed to determine whether there is any optimum size or distribution of settlement and to see how far this ideal pattern will need to be varied to meet particular local conditions. Whatever other outcome there might be, it seems clear from the decline in full-time agricultural employment, and other rural occupations, the problems of supplying services and facilities to the rural population, and the improvement in the standard of living achieved or expected by country people, that there are too many rural settlements, and most of these are too small. In purely economic terms, it seems that rural settlements are fast becoming both unnecessary and inefficient, and that as an urban society we should build no more villages, nor expand any country towns, but concentrate our efforts on large-scale expansions of the larger towns with highly sophisticated linear or grid forms of growth based on monorail or other means of fast transportation. Socially, because people wish to live in smaller communities and because some service centres are needed for farmers and others who must live in the country, rural settlement needs to be retained in some form, and the harsh test of economic viability and efficiency needs to be tempered by political, and therefore, social control. According to the 1964 *Analysis of the Survey for the Devonshire County Development Plan*, ' . . . the village as we know it has lost or is losing its economic raison d'étre', but 'compact rural settlements at a convenient distance from a town may provide a desirable alternative environment and way of life'. 'Employment opportunities to replace agricultural employment may best be provided . . . in key inland towns.'

In present-day town and country planning practice, the town map and its more recent counterpart, the urban structure map, have provided a reasonable basis for the preparation of detail plans in urban areas, even though, until recently, there have been no regional plans or studies from which to derive a sound economic base on which to build the town map. A very small part of the rural regions is covered by town maps, and for the rest—the great area of small towns, villages, hamlets, farms, fields and forests—there is no counterpart. In theory, all land is covered by some form of statutory plan, but for most rural areas the plan is the County Map, on a 1 inch to 1 mile base. The county map was designed to show the location of town maps, major road proposals and major land uses such as airfields and mineral workings (Map 9). Wide tracts of land were left unmarked. These became known as 'white land' through being un-coloured on the map. In 'white areas' the status quo was usually preserved by a statement of policy, that 'existing uses of land are intended to remain largely undisturbed'. At the 1965 Town and Country Planning Summer School, J. R. James, then Chief Planner to the Ministry of Housing and Local Government, expressed the view that

county maps . . . have proved to be of little value in setting out proposals, guiding developers or controlling development . . . their usefulness has been limited to illustrating county road patterns and acting as keys to town map submissions (by the local planning authorities to the Minister of Housing and Local Government) and the few areas to which areas of special policies of control applied.

Even where more forward-looking local planning authorities have sup-plemented their county maps by district or sub-regional proposals, these have been concerned mainly with the preservation of the countryside as a visual amenity, and with the projection of existing trends as a measure of the urban threat to rural peace: which leaves country planning a fairly undisturbed field of study so far as the future of settlement in the country-side is concerned.

At present, planning in the rural regions is practised at three levels, regional, county and town–village. This division is not entirely satis-factory. A better breakdown is obtained by defining regions, sub-regions, districts and localities, to which a corresponding scale of planning can be applied. In this book, the regional scale is taken to embrace the whole of each rural region. The sub-regions cover the major sub-divisions of the region, and may embrace a regional centre and its hinterland, for example

Exeter and the large surrounding area it serves, or a large area of similar character, such as the Lakes. The district scale covers the whole of a large town, or a grouping of smaller towns and villages, while the local scale includes individual villages, and parts of towns such as housing and industrial estates, or the town centre.

At a regional level, rural planning is concerned with the size, number and location of settlements, and their function. Regional planning techniques owe much to regional geography, and planners have made much use of the theories of 'settlement hierarchy' and 'central place'. In 'settlement hierarchy' theories, towns and villages are placed in order of size, or according to the facilities they provide. R. D. P. Smith's paper on the 'Changing Urban Hierarchy'[46] provides an example of a planner's use of this theory, to place towns and cities in an order of merit. The 'central place' theory relates the location of commercial and service centres to the distribution of surrounding settlements, density of population, and the distance people may have to travel to reach the centre. Population change and improved means of transport have been reflected in fewer centres, spaced farther apart. Associated with each centre is a 'service area' which surrounds the town, and from which the majority of people look to the town for their shopping, schooling and similar services. The application of these theories to planning is being challenged, because land-use transportation and other surveys are showing 'a more random and less predictable' pattern of movement than had been supposed.[47] Although people seem generally to look towards their nearest town, if they can obtain there the things they want, they are now exercising a greater degree of choice where they go, for example, combining shopping with family outings, in the car, with visits to other places. In the conurban regions, the number and proximity of centres makes it difficult to apply the settlement hierarchy—central place—service area theory with any firm meaning, but in the rural regions, where towns and villages are more regularly spaced, the continued application of these theories seems more justified. A hierarchy of dominant and intermediate centres and associated towns is illustrated in the *Regional Appraisal* of the East Anglia Consultative Committee,[48] and both the Committee and the Economic Planning Council accept this hierarchy as the basis for plans for the future growth of the region.

Planners claim that in trying to guide and control the pattern of settlement, one of their main objectives is to secure a wide range of facility

and service, and of employment and other opportunities. A useful sociological study could be made to see whether the standard of living and the
range of employment varies in any recognisable way with the size and
distribution of settlements. Planners usually assume that the larger the
settlement and the more concentrated the population in the surrounding
sub-region, the greater the range of opportunity it should be able to offer.
In vast conurbations, where traffic and transport are congested and costs
relatively high, there appears to be some limit to the extent to which
people take advantage of specialised and centrally placed facilities: in
which case, a proportionately greater population is needed to support,
say, a theatre in Birmingham or Manchester than one in Exeter or Shrews-
bury. Convenience of access may be as important as desire to participate in
assessing the potential of any regional centre. This may compensate par-
tially for the small total and sparse distribution of population in the rural
regions, which tend to limit the range of facilities the regional centres can
support. In contrast to the conurban regions, rural regions are characterised by small settlements with long lines of communication; advocates of
country life suggest that ease of movement compensates for greater distance and the closer network of community life in small settlements
compensates for having to travel to regional centres to satisfy all but local
needs. The sociologist may be able to assess the advantages and dis-
advantages of living in large and small settlements. He may also be able
to make an objective comparison between the quality of life in the
conurban and rural regions. He has not yet done so, but probably
because the case for this type of study has not yet been presented with
sufficient force.

For the present, argument about the relative merit of living in towns
and villages of different size and location will remain very subjective. In
the rural regions, plans should offer as wide a choice as economically
possible, but people choosing where to live should be reasonably clear
what each place may have to offer them. Commerce and industry are
well ahead of public authorities in studying consumer satisfaction, possibly
because authorities do not see the extent to which they are involved in
offering different commodities to the public, through their planning
policies. There is a need for studies of 'consumer satisfaction' in different
types and size of settlement, to measure both the provision of facilities
and the quality of social life against the expectation of the residents.

As with sociologists, economists seem to have had little to say about the relative efficiency of economic activity in large and small settlements, and in different regional situations. However, they have had rather more to say about settlement size and location where the development of new industry is concerned. The introduction of new industry has been an important part of Local Authority policy for the development of rural regions where employment opportunities have been shrinking, but economists have pointed to the need for large concentrations of population to attract and support industrial development, demonstrating how little industry the rural regions have been able to attract unless development has been artificially stimulated from nearby conurbations by financial incentive through the development of new towns or town expansion schemes. D. I. MacKay and W. F. Luttrell, speaking at a conference of the Regional Studies Association and the Town Planning Institute at Cambridge in January, 1968, supported the hypothesis that large concentrations of population were needed to support the 'viable economic, self-supporting development of industry', varying between 200,000 for 'towns of a size to take a great deal of industry on a full-scale factory basis' and 500,000, where there could be a labour market capable of acting 'as a counter-magnet to London'. There is no single concentration of half-a-million people in the rural regions and only 1 town of more than 200,000.

By the same token—the need for large concentrations of population—it is argued that only the subsidiary elements in manufacturing industry, and the smallest and therefore the most vulnerable branches, are established in rural areas. These do not provide a sound basis for the rural economy and it is no solution to replace lost agricultural employment by the introduction of small industrial concerns, the majority of which employ female labour. This argument against small industrial centres was being advanced in economic circles at a time when the planners in the Ministry of Housing and Local Government were advising a change in Government policy, away from small town expansion schemes. Until the mid-sixties, most of the town expansion schemes were in the order of 10,000 to 20,000 population with corresponding industrial development. Since then, much larger schemes have been promoted, such as at Peterborough, where a population increase of 70,000 is planned. Town expansion is now seen on a scale equivalent to the original (1946–50) new towns around London, and new towns are correspondingly larger. The implication seems to be that a rural region wishing to offer accommodation for population from an overcrowded conurbation must accept either the large-scale expansion of its major cities or the addition of a large new town, and may no longer look towards a solution of its own problems by the more modest expansion of a number of smaller country towns. An exception is to be found in mid-Wales, where the proposal by Economic Associates Ltd.[49] for a new town of 60,000 to 70,000 people at Caersws and Newtown, has been toned down (in the first stage) to a doubling of the population of Newtown (i.e. an increase of 5,500 persons in a period of 7-10 years).[50]

Most planned expansion, whether in new towns or by town expansion schemes, has been in the conurban regions (Map 8). However, the Greater London Council's town expansion programme has extended into the south central and eastern rural regions, with a number of small expansion schemes in small country towns. Taken together, these schemes have made a noticeable contribution to London's accommodation problem; individually they have contributed to the prosperity of each town and its surrounding villages. It is not clear why small town expansion schemes are out of favour with the Government. They may be more difficult to implement, but they seem to cost no more than the large schemes such as Milton Keynes, New Town, designed to accommodate a quarter of a million people at an estimated cost of £700 million, or nearly £3,000 per person. The Mid-Wales Development Corporation estimate the cost of the Newtown expansion at £11 million, or £2,000 per person accommodated. While the larger scheme may offer more by way of facilities and services, and in its industrial growth potential, the smaller town expansion offers a viable alternative, and still has a valid place in regional plans. Yet, outside Wales, Economic Planning Council's studies and reports seem to offer little prospect of expansion in the rural regions outside the major regional centres, and the prospect for the smaller towns and remote areas is not good. The Hunt Committee on the 'Intermediate Areas'[51] considered the problems of the rural regions, in areas where employment opportunities were declining, but their terms of reference drew their attention towards the more acute problems of the conurban regions. In the rural regions, only the Plymouth area was thought to warrant special assistance of subsidy. Elsewhere, the Hunt Committee accepted the view, expressed by the East Anglia Economic Planning Council, that local action to stimulate the growth of a few selected centres would suffice. Neither the Committee nor the Planning Council gave any indication how many centres should be developed, or how their development should be stimulated, but a study is being made

of the needs, prospects and potential of small country towns by the East
Anglia Economic Planning Board and the East Anglia Consultative Committee, and this may provide some useful guidance.

Unless some positive action is taken to alter them, the trends evident
over the last 15–20 years will probably continue, the regional pattern of
development being growth in the main centres, at the relative, or real
expense of the more remote and smaller villages, and a slow but unsteady
growth in most larger villages and in the small and medium sized towns.
The planner too often sees this only in terms of a changing hierarchy of
centres, with some centres gaining over the others in function and in their
area of influence. He can assess and project trends on a regional scale, but
he lacks the tools and methodology to make an effective assessment of the
social and economic needs of a rural region or to carry out a policy which
anticipates a different level of growth from that shown by the trend.
The planner normally converts the projected trend into a regional programme, but because the trend is so uncertain, and to meet the possibility
of changing circumstances, he writes the uncertainty into the plan as
flexibility. Thus, the plan period is elastic, and programmes of investment
are interchangeable.

Regional Economic Planning Councils have included broad structure
plans in their reports, giving the Council's view of future changes in the
settlement pattern. These plans cover the standard regions and are therefore more concerned with the major conurbations than with the rural
regions. Nevertheless, they indicate fairly strongly the belief that by far
the greatest part of any future investment and expansion will be in the
major urban centres, and that the rural areas do not raise particularly in-
tractible problems. County Planning Authorities probably see rural
regional problems as more serious, and pay more attention to them,
particularly where there are regional groupings or 'conferences' of the
authorities.

In their *Regional Appraisal*[52] the East Anglia Consultative Committee
noted that the dominant regional centres—Norwich, Cambridge, Ipswich
and Peterborough—and their surrounding commuter zones would continue to attract most of the new development (unless there were a fundamental change in government policy). The intermediate towns, such as
King's Lynn, Bury St Edmunds, Great Yarmouth, Lowestoft and Felixstowe, would also continue to grow, but the Committee noted with some
concern the wide belt of land containing many hundreds of small settle-

ments, towns and villages, in which problems of 'remoteness, sparse or falling population, and lack of social and economic opportunities' had still to be faced. Further studies of the problem of growth and decline in the region are expected from both the Consultative Committee and the Economic Planning Council, and similar studies should be forthcoming for other rural regions from the other regional organisations. But both the groupings of local planning authorities and the economic planning councils are advisory bodies; formal (i.e. statutory) planning has been practised by individual counties and county boroughs, which constitute the planning authorities under the planning acts of 1947–68. County planning approximates to a sub-regional level of planning, although most counties are not well composed as planning sub-regions.

Sub-regional planning differs from regional in degree as much as in content. Like regional planning it is concerned with the size and spatial distribution of settlement, but where the regional plan is concerned mainly with a strategy for economic and social development (i.e. with regional roles, levels of growth and the strategic distribution of population on a wide scale), in planning a sub-region the physical structure of settlement is a much more important factor. The inadequacy of the county map as a statement of sub-regional policy[53] has been recognised by both central and local government authorities. The County plan gives little indication of the planning authority's intentions about the future structure of settlement.[54] In recent years, sub-regional studies have been promoted by more forward-looking authorities, to deal with the problems of growth round the major centres, but in most parts of the rural regions, county planning has extended little beyond a local ordering of the growth of each town and rural district. Rather than prepare sub-regional plans, most authorities in the rural regions have relied on their general knowledge of their area to see that plans for individual towns and villages have made collective sense.

The structure plans which will replace the County Map, when the Town and Country Planning Act, 1968, is brought into effect,[55] will require very much more of local planning authorities. The structure plan will be a largely written document supported by diagrams, explaining how the planning authority intends moulding the pattern of employment, housing and communications taking into account the likely rate of investment in the sub-region. The plans prepared under the 1947–62 Acts indicated a pattern of land uses and communications, to be achieved within a twenty-year period. The new type of plan will be less closely tied to a land use projection; instead it will combine a land use and transportation structure with a development programme and policy statement. As with the 1947–62 Acts, the Planning Authority has to demonstrate that it has carried out a survey, but the new Act requires that they publish the survey, and consider a variety of possibilities before making any firm decision on the plan. It is doubtful whether rural planning practice, or theory, have advanced sufficiently for planning authorities in the rural regions to prepare structure plans as envisaged in the new Act. Techniques have not yet been developed, either to test different rural settlement structures, or to relate rural development proposals to the likely future level of investment.

In the conurban regions, resources are being devoted to the application of new techniques to structure plans, and local planning authorities are working with the Centre for Environmental Studies and other research organisations. A number of sub-regional studies have been published, notably the South Hampshire, Leicester and Leicestershire, and Notts and Derby studies, which indicate a more objective approach to sub-regional planning, and which show how new techniques of analysis may be used to test the impact of various development possibilities and programmes. These new techniques should result in much more efficient programmes of development which will secure considerable savings in capital expenditure on schools, highways and sewerage, to take but three examples. The saving should greatly exceed the outlay to support the necessary research, and to purchase computer time. But, in the rural regions, there seems to be less understanding of the value of the new techniques, or, possibly, an unwillingness to devote the slender resources of the planning authorities to methods which have not been completely accepted. But without a more comprehensive system of data collection and analysis, and more refined methods for testing plan possibilities, there is a very real danger that the structure plans in the rural regions will be no more than the old development plans dressed up in a new guise. Authorities in eight areas are being invited to prepare the first of the new structure plans. Seven of the areas are in the conurban regions, but one, embracing the County of Norfolk and the City of Norwich, is in a rural region. What these two authorities achieve may set the standard for other rural sub-regions.

One of the most intransigent problems facing planners in the rural regions has been the division between county and county borough councils, dividing responsibility for sub-regional planning between authorities with very different viewpoints, and with a vested interest in representing town and country interests as something very far apart. It has been an achievement when plans on either side of the county–county borough boundary have fitted together in detail; it is seldom that they have been together in objectives or policies.

If the Royal Commission proposals for provincial councils are eventually accepted the Economic Planning Councils will hand over to Councils with full responsibility for economic and physical planning, and there will be a statutory authority for regional planning. The proposed Unitary authorities will then be able to prepare sub-regional structure plans within a firmer regional framework than is available to the local planning authorities from the Economic Planning Councils today.

Planning policy in the rural regions needs to be interpreted at a district level, between the sub-regional structure and local plans. The District scale of planning covers the larger town, the smaller town and its surrounding villages and groups of villages, not necessarily related to a single country town, but with similar planning problems. Under the Planning Acts of 1947 to 1962, the most common form of district plan was the town map, a formal plan which had to be approved by the Minister of Housing and Local Government before it could be added to the statutory development plan. In the rural regions, where a large number of towns are small, formal town maps have been approved for towns as small as 10,000–20,000 population. The town map has been much criticised, being a rather crude tool with which to handle the complexities of the towns which make up the large conurbations. But for the comparatively simple problems encountered in country towns, the town map has proved more suitable. Nevertheless, the formality of the town map, with its quasi-legal definition of land uses, can profitably give way to the more flexible form of plan envisaged in the new Act.

Some local planning authorities have prepared village development policy statements and plans on a comprehensive basis for complete rural districts,[56] but rural district boundaries frequently divide villages and hamlets where there is considerable inter-play of social and economic activity, and group settlements where there are considerable differences. Although politically convenient, rural district council areas do not usually form satisfactory units for preparing or presenting district plans. Even if taken together, town maps for country towns and the adjoining rural district policy maps do not add up to effective district plans in the rural sub-regions. This is partly because of the areas they cover, but also because the plan and policy content is weak. Surprisingly little attention has been given, even by planners working in rural counties, to the content of district plans, apart from the concept that they should indicate key villages, road proposals and development control policies limiting areas for development, e.g. mineral reserves and areas of high amenity value. District plans are probably the most critical in achieving positive planning in the rural regions. They should illustrate:

(1) The application of policies outlined in the sub-regional plan to hamlets, villages and towns.

(2) The location of areas for new development and redevelopment, and the level of growth anticipated in each settlement in the district.

(3) Proposed improvements in the communications network.

(4) How public transport services in the district will be operated, and on what primary routes.

(5) A programme of investment in social and commercial facilities and public services (including some indication of village school closures).

Under the New Act, structure maps are to be prepared for towns of 50,000 population or more, and informal plans for towns of a lesser size. The structure maps will be submitted for approval to the Minister of Housing and Local Government; the informal plans will be approved only by the local planning authority. There are relatively few towns of over 50,000 population in the rural regions, and very many smaller towns and villages. District plans will therefore be very much a local concern, whether the plans cover the development of single, larger settlements, or groups of smaller ones.[57]

District plans in this form will translate sub-regional structure into specific proposals, will give a realistic assessment of the potential for growth in individual settlements and the level of investment likely in public and private enterprise. They will give firm guide lines against which more detailed local planning can proceed. The lack of satisfactory district plans has inhibited the preparation of local plans in rural areas, particularly where there has been uncertainty about the level and distribution of growth and the future pattern of services and facilities.

The local plan can take many forms: the most common are the village plan, the small town centre plan, the residential development—or re-

Plate 1 (*a*) The opening up of fields and the persistent removal of hedge-row trees (*b*) Parkland under the plough—islands of trees, but how long will they remain?

a

b

a

b

Plate 3 New estates in old villages (*a*) Undisguised suburbia (*b*) Landscaped higher income commuter

a

b

Plate 4 Attractive centres of small country towns planned to become 'pedestrian only'

Plate 5 (*a*) Street scheduled for widening to provide traffic circulation round pedestrian shopping centre (*b*) Area to be cleared for car parking, according to approved plan

a

b

Plate 6 (*a*) Rear service behind new central area development, and ramp to roof car park (*b*) Rear service, provided to existing properties, revealing some of the problems of adaptation

a

- b

Plate 7 Industrial enterprise in small country towns (*a*) An individual site being developed by a single large firm operating on the outskirts of the town (*b*) Access into a Council industrial area

a

b

Plate 8 Town Development Act: expansion on a large scale in a small town (*a*) Housing and industry (in the background) (*b*) In the same town, new riverside shopping and car park

a

b

Plate 9 (*a*) Coastal caravan site (*b*) The caravan is giving way to the chalet

a

b

Plate 10 A major power development: North Sea Gas coastal installations

Map 1 Rural regions

Transitional Zone between conurban and rural regions

① North England & South Scotland
② East England & East Anglia
③ Wales & the West Country
④ South Central England
⑤ South West England

Map 2 Rural regions—the changing situation

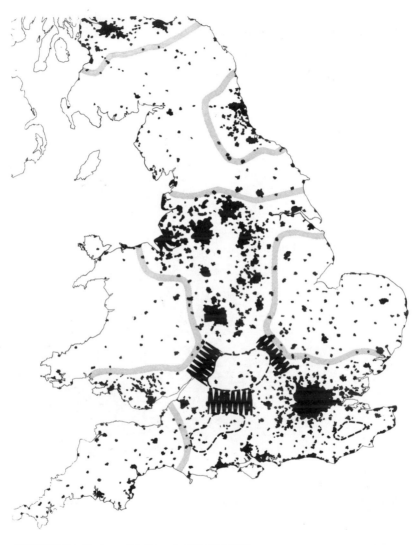

Transitional zones between rural and conurban regions
Motorway zones of conurban growth
Intermediate rural areas within the major conurban region

Map 3 Rural regions and economic planning regions

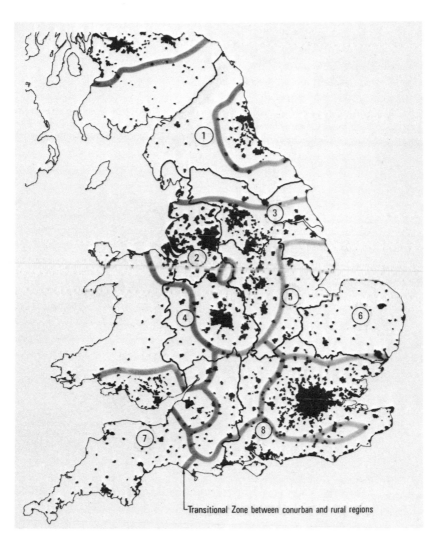

Transitional Zone between conurban and rural regions

① Northern
② North Western
③ Yorkshire & Humberside
④ West Midland
⑤ East Midland
⑥ East Anglia
⑦ South Western
⑧ South Eastern

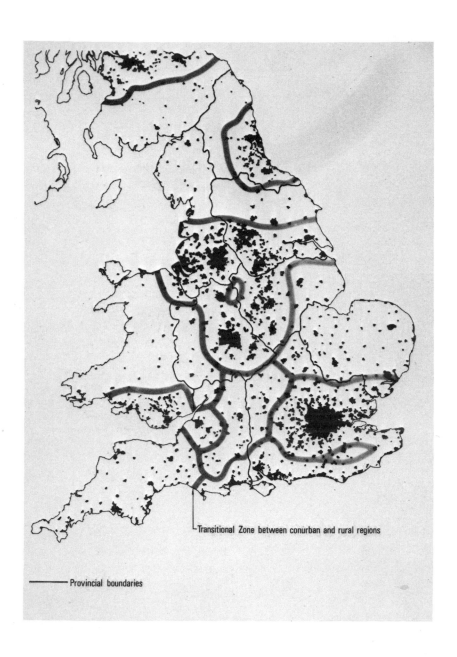

Transitional Zone between conurban and rural regions

Provincial boundaries

Map 5 Rural and conurban provinces

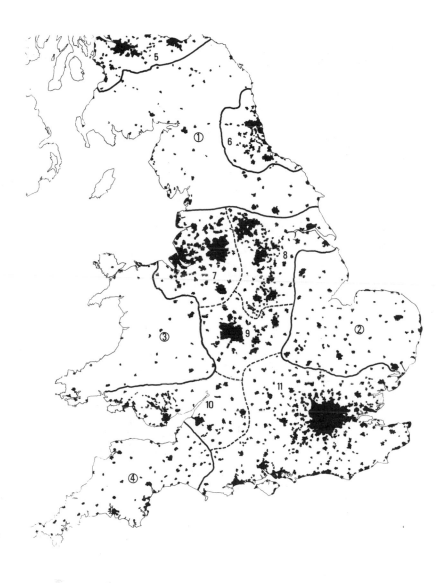

① Northern England & Southern Scotland   7 Mersey – Manchester
② East & East Anglia   8 West Yorkshire & Humber
③ Wales & The Black Country   9 Midlands
④ South West England   10 Bristol & South Wales
5 Firth/Clyde   11 London & South Coast
6 Tyne – Tees

Map 6 East Anglia—rates of growth and decline

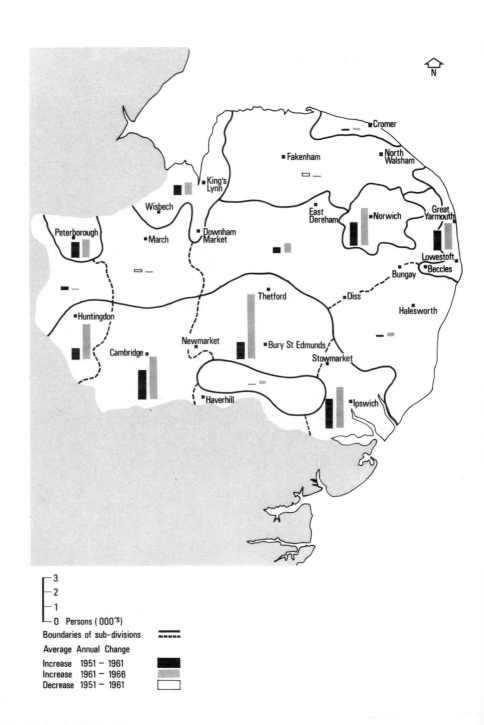

N

3
2
1
0 Persons (000's)
Boundaries of sub-divisions
Average Annual Change
Increase 1951 − 1961
Increase 1961 − 1966
Decrease 1951 − 1961

Map 7 Motorway proposals and the rural regions

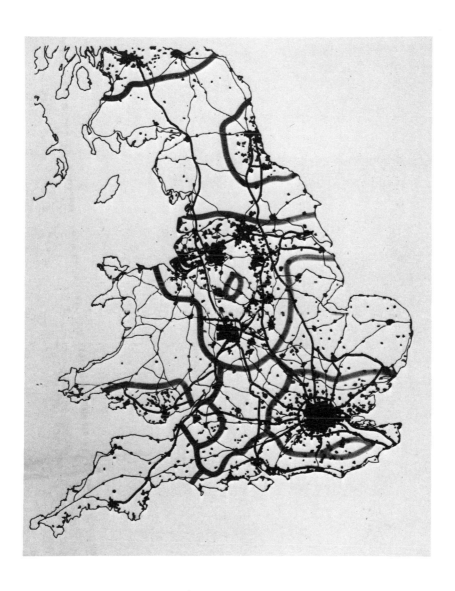

Motorways and other roads to be substantially improved by the mid 1970's

Other "trunk roads"

Map 8 New and expanding towns and the rural regions

New Towns
Expanding Towns

Map 9 County map extract

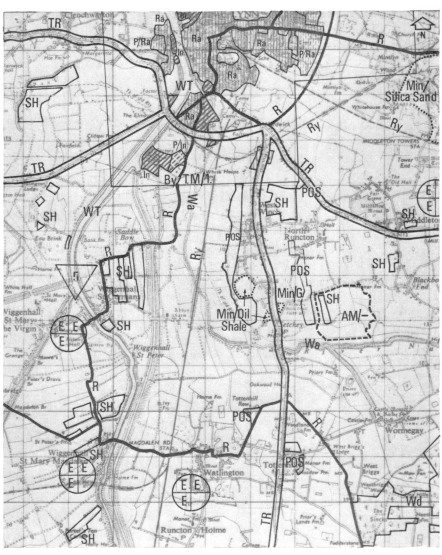

Area comprised in Town Map	By TM	Primary school	
Existing industrial area		Clinic	
Proposed industrial area		Village hall	
Existing built up area		Area for which a designation	
Proposed development		map has been approved	
Service department area		Areas intended for	WD/-
Small-holdings	SH	mineral workings	

Public Open Space	POS		
Woodland	Wd		
Water	Wa		
Trunk roads			
Principal roads			
Waterways	WT		
Railways	Ry		

Map 10 Felixstowe town map

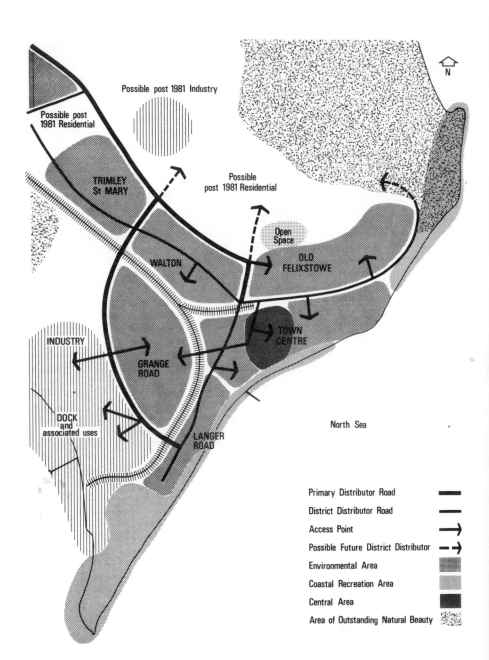

N

Possible post 1981 Industry

Possible post 1981 Residential

TRIMLEY St MARY

Possible post 1981 Residential

WALTON

Open Space

OLD FELIXSTOWE

INDUSTRY

GRANGE ROAD

TOWN CENTRE

DOCK and associated uses

LANGER ROAD

North Sea

Primary Distributor Road

District Distributor Road

Access Point

Possible Future District Distributor

Environmental Area

Coastal Recreation Area

Central Area

Area of Outstanding Natural Beauty

Map 11 Dorchester town map

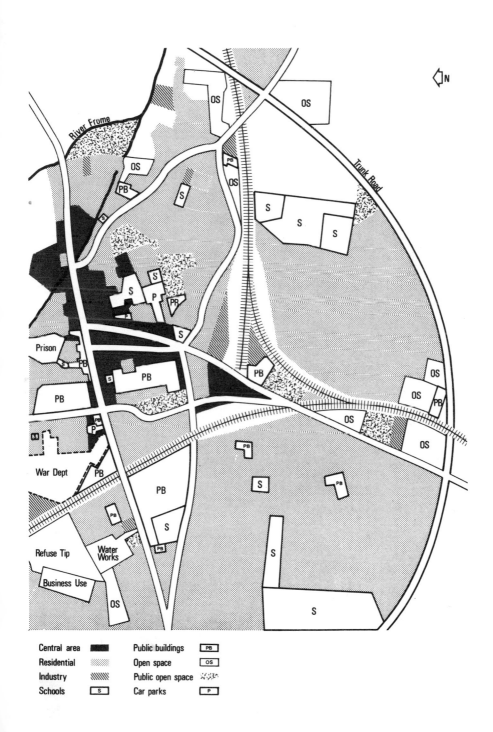

Central area
Residential
Industry
Schools

Public buildings
Open space
Public open space
Car parks

Map 12 East Retford policy

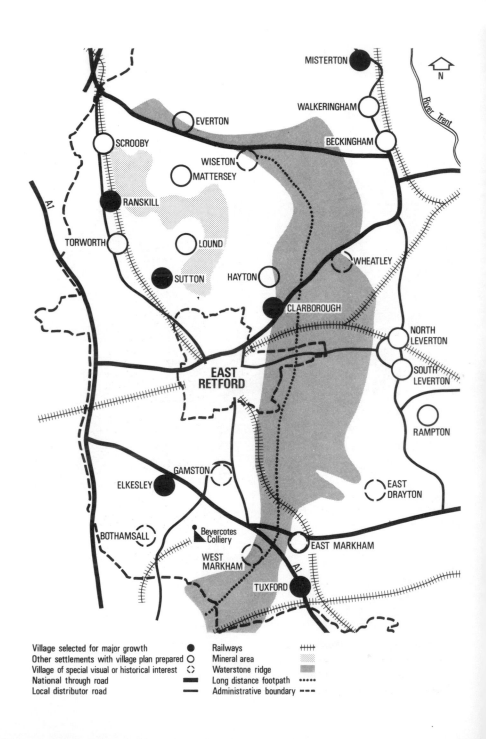

N

Village selected for major growth ● Railways ++++
Other settlements with village plan prepared ○ Mineral area
Village of special visual or historical interest ◇ Waterstone ridge
National through road ▬ Long distance footpath •••••
Local distributor road ▬ Administrative boundary ---

Map 13 Gayton village plan

Existing built up area	School	Vehicle access point
New residential development	Proposed school extension	
Area for shops, etc.	New public open space	
Area of particular character	Footpaths	

Map 14 Brampton central area proposals

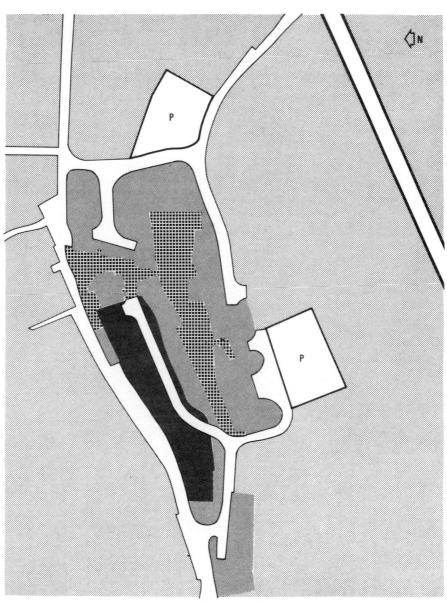

Existing centre
Redevelopment area
Pedestrian areas
By-pass
Service roads
Car parks

Map 15 Truro town centre map

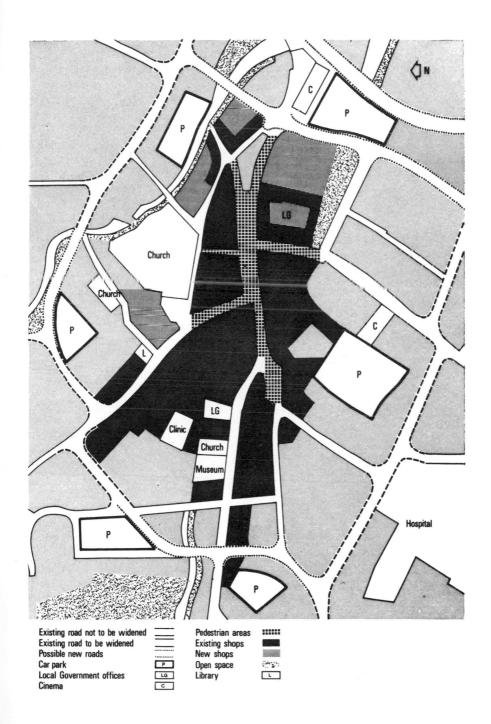

Existing road not to be widened

Existing road to be widened

Possible new roads

Car park — P

Local Government offices — LG

Cinema — C

Pedestrian areas

Existing shops

New shops

Open space

Library — L

Map 16 Recreation areas and the rural regions

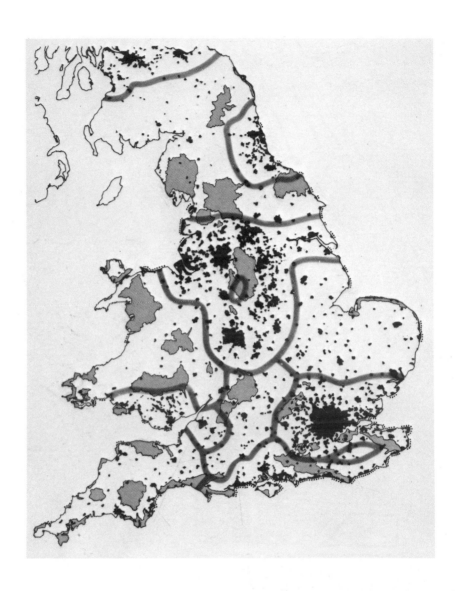

······ Main holiday coastline
National Parks
Areas of Outstanding Natural Beauty

Map 17 Structure plans and the rural regions

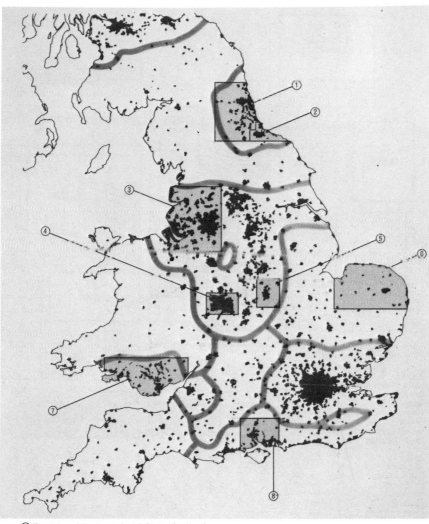

① Tyneside and Northumberland & Durham (coalfield)
② Teesside
③ Lancashire, Liverpool, Manchester & Cheshire
④ Birmingham, Wolverhampton & The Black Country
⑤ Leicester & Leicestershire
⑥ Norwich & Norfolk
⑦ Southampton, Portsmouth & Hampshire
⑧ Glamorgan & Monmouthshire

Diagram A typical small town centre

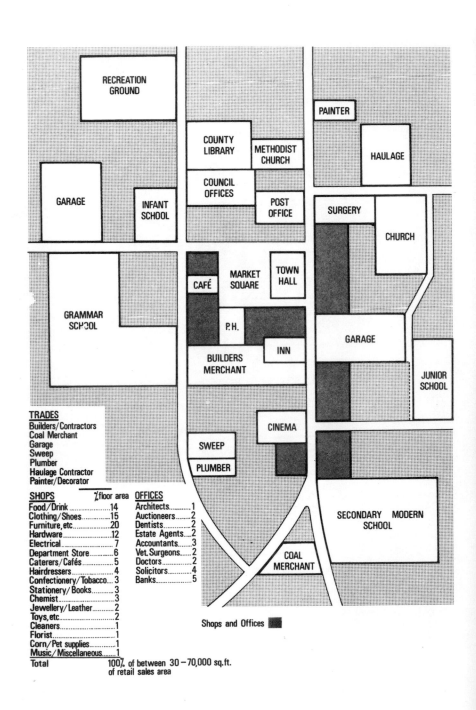

RECREATION GROUND

PAINTER

COUNTY LIBRARY

METHODIST CHURCH

HAULAGE

GARAGE

INFANT SCHOOL

COUNCIL OFFICES

POST OFFICE

SURGERY

CHURCH

CAFÉ

MARKET SQUARE

TOWN HALL

GRAMMAR SCHOOL

P.H.

BUILDERS MERCHANT

INN

GARAGE

JUNIOR SCHOOL

CINEMA

SWEEP

PLUMBER

SECONDARY MODERN SCHOOL

COAL MERCHANT

TRADES
Builders/Contractors
Coal Merchant
Garage
Sweep
Plumber
Haulage Contractor
Painter/Decorator

SHOPS	% floor area
Food/Drink	14
Clothing/Shoes	15
Furniture, etc	20
Hardware	12
Electrical	7
Department Store	6
Caterers/Cafés	5
Hairdressers	4
Confectionery/Tobacco	3
Stationery/Books	3
Chemist	3
Jewellery/Leather	2
Toys, etc	2
Cleaners	1
Florist	1
Corn/Pet supplies	1
Music/Miscellaneous	1
Total	100% of between 30 – 70,000 sq.ft. of retail sales area

OFFICES	
Architects	1
Auctioneers	2
Dentists	2
Estate Agents	2
Accountants	3
Vet. Surgeons	2
Doctors	2
Solicitors	4
Banks	5

Shops and Offices ■

development—area, and even amongst these local plans there are many variations of form and presentation. There has been a tendency, in the past, to prepare local plans showing in great detail proposals where there was no great likelihood that development would be carried out, or where there were not the means to implement or enforce the plan. Authorities have wasted considerable effort on abortive local planning, but the lesson is being learnt and a greater sense of realism seems to be creeping in to local plans prepared by planning authorities. Of all the settlements in the rural regions, the greatest attention has probably been given by County Planning Departments to the village plan; these fall into three general groups:

(1) The conservation plan, designed primarily to protect a village from the intrusion of the 'wrong' type of building; these plans are based on a largely physical and architectural study of the existing village.

(2) The land-use plan for the expanding village; these plans usually follow an intensive and detailed survey of the social and physical structure of the village, including a study of expansion potential (which would have been made as part of a district survey had there been a district plan). In the result, which may include a structure of roads and footpaths as well as a land-use pattern, most of the social survey is not apparent, largely because it is usually irrelevant to the type of plan produced.

(3) The outline plan, embodying a structure of roads and footpaths, indicating land for specific purposes such as schools and open spaces, but leaving the question of land use largely to be determined by future events, guided by development control policy.

Combinations of the three forms of plan are made where circumstances require.

Funds for the improvement of the village road pattern by the highway authority are likely to be in short supply; similarly, the number of villages where the plans contain by-pass proposals likely to be implemented in the next 10 to 15 years is strictly limited by economic circumstance, particularly when compared with the number of villages where through traffic warrants a by-pass. Although village planning has held such pride of place amongst country planners, both in their practical work, and in their discussions, there is still needed a technique by which a realistic assessment of economic potential can be introduced into village plans and by which it is possible to distinguish between those elements of the plan which are enforceable by the local planning authority and those

E

which are purely advisory; this would draw public attention to the local planning authority's limited powers in compelling developers and occupiers of property to follow the ideas expounded in the plan.

Another difficult problem in village planning is the relatively poor quality of new residential building, and in particular, the introduction of estate development, breaking up the scale of the old village, and introducing into it the aesthetics of the suburb. Highway requirements, and the policy of concentrating new development into larger expansions of selected villages, have been largely responsible for the estates of bungalows and chalet-houses which have been added to so many villages, and they continue to pose a very difficult problem. Although much has been written, and said, about the particular requirements of building in villages, and the older and more attractive parts of country towns, detail plans in rural areas seem to differ little from urban, the rural entrepreneur apparently sees rural requirements as much the same as urban—and there is surprisingly little difference between building in the conurbations outside the main centres, and building in rural regions. Most planning authorities are now well aware of the problems and seek a solution either by preparing very detailed plans defining road alignments, footpaths, open spaces and even suggesting the siting of houses, or by preparing outline plans which define blocks of land for development, each related to the overall plan by specific landscape and open space proposals as well as by an outline of the road and footpath system. Whichever form of village plan is adopted, the result will depend largely on the ability of the developer's architect.

A special study is needed of the problems involved in financing and implementing village plans and of the impact of estate development in villages, especially those where the local planning authority is guiding development on a relatively large scale. These studies could possibly be undertaken by the Countryside Commission as a natural extension to their work.

The type of plan needed to guide estate development round country towns also needs study. Being small the country town generally offers a good chance of integrating new development into the old pattern, and some of the town expansion schemes in small towns round London and the other conurbations, give an indication of how this can be achieved, but it should be remembered that these town development schemes are designed mainly for people who are not usually in a position to buy their way into the owner-occupier class and who must therefore accept what the planner thinks is good for them. Many move to town expansion areas to leave overcrowded and unsatisfactory conditions in the conurbations and the Council needs to take little account of what their tenants would choose, if they could afford to purchase their own house. Nevertheless, there are a number of schemes, some prepared by local authority architects and planners, some by planners and architects in private practice, which make a major contribution in the field of small town planning.

The slum clearance programme in the rural regions is probably no less, proportionately, than in the conurbations, but sub-standard housing in rural areas is generally more scattered and there are few areas of potential redevelopment. However, in most country towns, mainly in or near the town centres, and in some villages, areas have been defined for redevelopment, sometimes for residential redevelopment, but also for commercial use, or for car parking. Redevelopment proposals normally form part of village plans or town centre maps, but because of the limited economic potential, the rate of redevelopment or commercial expansion is usually very slow. The centres of most country towns are worth conserving, either for the buildings themselves or for the street pattern and the spaces it forms, and a fairly standard form of town centre plan has been evolved to preserve the 'historic' centre while taking advantage of surrounding areas of vacant land, slum clearance and other outworn property, to provide space for rear servicing for shops, distributor roads and car parks. Town centre maps for towns in the rural regions usually contain four main features:

(1) A pedestrian shopping centre, based mainly on the existing pattern of streets, but usually containing at least one small proposal for expansion.

(2) Car parking at ground level only.

(3) Rear service roads.

(4) Other new roads where needed to accommodate traffic removed from the centre when made traffic-free.

These plans generally seem satisfactory, but they are relatively expensive, and their implementation would seem to depend primarily on the direction of car-parking revenues into central area development.

Where plans have not been prepared, either for the lack of staff, or because the local planning authority have not shown any desire to prepare local plans, stop-gap measures, in the form of village envelopes and urban limit maps, have been taken to guide developers and illustrate policy.

The envelope is formed by a line defining the boundary between the village and the surrounding open country. It is used by local planning authorities to give detail meaning to their policy that new development should not normally be permitted outside the existing village envelope (in conformity to Ministry of Housing and Local Government's Houses in the Country policy). In some counties, the village envelope has been adapted to implement a slightly more sophisticated policy, aimed at the selection of villages for expansion, by varying the amount of open land within the envelope according to the amount of development it is desired to attract. Near the larger cities and towns, even within rural regions, the effect of including land within a village envelope seems much the same as allocating it specifically for residential development and a village plan would be better than a village envelope. However, in other parts of the rural regions, where the demand for housing is much less, the village envelope has given a choice of sites where building is likely to be permitted within a village. The urban limit map adopts the village envelope technique and applies it to small towns to define areas for new development. The urban limit map has also been used to define land for specific functions, such as schools, industry, roads and pedestrian routes. In the rural regions, the village envelope and town limit maps can become useful tools for the local planner, by showing the range of possible sites available to builders and to the public generally; where demand is lower than availability, they give a desirable element of flexibility.

In large parts of the countryside, the criteria for deciding whether or not development should be permitted has been its relation to the existing pattern rather than to any future plan, and this is by no means illogical in the more remote areas, or in the smaller villages where the rate of development is low and where the choice of land suitable for building is great. In these areas, statements of policy related to the siting of buildings are generally of greater value than a plan in the usual 'land use' sense.

7 Local environment
and landscape

In the smaller country towns, and in most villages, there is little opportunity for local planning authorities to stimulate change by positive action. Apart from a small amount of council house building, which is the responsibility of district councils rather than the county council, almost all the initiative lies with private enterprise and the function of the local planning authority is to guide rather than to sponsor. However desirable it might be to build up the size of one settlement, or reduce the size of another, this can be done only by rejecting any proposals contrary to local policy, and accepting those which conform. The executive powers of the county councils are restricted generally to the provision of schools and highways, and the giving of grants towards some other facilities, and co-ordination between highways, education and planning committees is by no means to be taken for granted. The implementing authority for many plans in rural regions is the district council;[58] thus, local planning with the County Council as local planning authority, is largely advisory, and lacks adequate power for positive action.

Both the majority report of the Royal Commission on Local Government in England, and Derek Senior's minority report, accepted the need for larger units of local government, with correspondingly greater financial support. This should make for greater efficiency, but it will not increase the total income or expenditure per person in the enlarged area. It could have the effect of concentrating expenditure into a relatively few expanding settlements, leaving the remainder, and particularly the more remote, even worse off. It is a strange anomaly, that urban and rural district councils, whose income is relatively low, because of the low product of the penny rate, should have such limited means to improve towns and villages, while agriculture, subsidised and protected, is still exempt from rates, and makes no direct contribution to either the upkeep of the services it uses, such as roads, or to the general welfare of the district.

Local planning authorities have had a fair measure of success in guiding development to conform to their local policies, mainly through the application of their powers of development control, and the pattern of development in and around most country towns and villages has been logical, if uninspired. The danger of accepting proposals which make neat patterns on plans, rather than something sensible on the ground has not always been avoided, a result of the inadequate training of some planning staff, the lack of interest on the part of many members of planning committees and poor detail plans for newly developing areas, both in towns and villages. Tidyness in the pattern of development seems to have been the watchword of most local planning authorities, with a considerable emphasis on the implementation of specific highway standards rather than the achievement of a satisfactory local environment as a whole.

Outside the planning and associated professions, town and country planning is probably judged more by its results at district and local level of town plan and village and housing layout than by any sub-regional and regional achievements. Many people, looking at the estates of detached and semi-detached houses and bungalows which surround the towns, and which have intruded into the village scene, wonder what is really achieved by the elaborate system of planning control. Certainly town and country planning can take credit for preventing sporadic building in the countryside (although much of the charm of the countryside derives from the presence of individual residences, farmhouses and cottages, set in farmland). Planning has prevented ribbon development along country lanes, has helped preserve some of the older parts of towns and villages from redevelopment, and saved much good quality farmland by guiding development onto poorer land. Most towns have had the benefit of a 'plan' of some sort to guide their growth and planning can add to its credit list the new towns and the expanding towns, which offer a safe, convenient and pleasant environment in which to live.

But few of the major achievements of British town and country planning lie in the rural regions; by contrast with the conurban regions, there is little to show for all the years of effort, and the question arises how much abortive effort is involved in the planning process in the rural regions.

The most positive thinking by country planners about village and small town planning includes traffic and pedestrian separation in residential and shopping areas, comprehensive estate development and similar concepts evolved out of urban—and mainly conurban—problems and conditions; whether their application to rural planning will be accepted by either the local authorities or the public still remains to be seen in most areas.

More often than not, detailed layouts have failed to take advantage of the overall pattern which has been laid down because:

(a) by far the greater amount of new development is dull and mono-tonous, and layout and individual house design is singularly lacking in inspiration;

(b) many layouts approved by local planning authorities lack either open space or provision for planting trees;

(c) the lack of footpaths, linking culs-de-sac, loop roads, etc., means that hundreds of yards are added to each walk to and from schools, shops, and bus stops.

Many authorities employ architects to improve the design of buildings for which planning permission is being sought, but this only removes the worst excesses of builders who do not employ architects, and protects the architecturally conservative authority from the more exuberant efforts of young designers with new ideas. In some authorities, assistants who are not architects find themselves employed in 'improving' submitted designs, with somewhat dubious results. It is not unknown for what can only be described as a mild form of coercion to be employed in persuading a stubborn applicant to see the planners' light by the utterance of such phrases as 'I doubt the committee will accept it like that' or, 'the com-mittee do not normally approve houses without chimneys'. There are few examples of good new building in the rural regions, either in villages or in country towns. It is worth looking at the new buildings which have attracted Civic Design awards to see which are considered by architects and planners to be above average, and to compare them with the typical houses and bungalows in small gardens with individual vehicular access to individual garages which appears to be what most people accept, if not demand. In the rural regions the civic design awards have gone generally to town expansion scheme houses, factories and shopping groups designed by architects to meet the special requirements of particular customers, usually corporations or companies rather than individual people.

Planners and architects in the rural regions—as in the conurbations—have advocated the building of terrace houses, open front gardens, grouped garages, limited vehicular access to houses, separate footpaths and various degrees of Radburn layout, but this advocacy has generally failed. Some Councils have built in this form on the advice of their own architects and planners (who generally fail to practise what they preach because they live in large individual houses set in their own, large gardens), but few private builders have moved away from the conventional. Planners have also advocated the provision of small open spaces within residential areas for local community use, but difficulties have usually been raised about financing and maintaining these areas, and, even where the land is left open, it is seldom developed properly as an open space.

Most people take great care with their houses and gardens, and, although the standard of design in and round the house is not high, this is not so much for the lack of concern, but for the lack of education in aesthetics. Yet even the care which is shown within the curtilage of the house is seldom repeated by local authorities and statutory undertakers in their control of the immediate surroundings. Trees are unnecessarily felled or are badly lopped, lovely old features are removed to make way for nothing very worthwhile or even for something positively ugly, and few people complain. The art of building in country towns and villages seems to have been lost, and planning control is not able to restore it. In many places, amenity societies have been formed to stimulate local interest in improving the environs of village, suburb and town. These societies are often led by local architects and have assumed the role of enlightened public watchdog, but while they are doing excellent work, and some are making a positive contribution by helping local authorities by carrying out survey and offering constructive criticism, others are inclined to blame authorities for all that goes wrong, regardless where the fault may really lie. They are sometimes critical of the professional advice given to authorities by their officers, and sometimes this criticism is unjustified. Nevertheless, many planning officers seem more concerned with efficiency in the routine and procedures of planning administration than with the quality of their proposals or recommendations, and many local councils, to whom development control powers are delegated by county planning authorities,[58] are more concerned with seeing houses, factories and schools, etc., built, than with the particular planning tasks with which Parliament has entrusted them. With the uninspired layouts they see for most of the time and the uninspired advice they so often receive from their advisors they can hardly be blamed. Yet, the responsibility for what is being permitted is theirs; the planning officers are only their paid advisors, and if their advice is unsound—or sound but rejected—they have only themselves to blame, and the electors who put their councillors in that position by their vote or their apathy cannot escape their share of the blame.

When the majority of people want imaginative development and re-development they will get it; in the meantime, it is a long uphill struggle for the country planner who thinks that country planning should bring as much benefit to the rural regions as to the conurbations; and in the meantime a generally low standard of building and layout will prevail.

The greatest visual problem confronting the country planner derives from the immense increase in the scale of human activity, an increase which is seen in the rate of building operations as well as in the size of individual projects. Planners in the rural regions have had something of a pre-occupation with the new technological developments in power and communications, visually apparent in power lines, radio masts and aerials, motorways and airfields, and, most recently, in the North Sea Gas termini. At Bacton, in Norfolk, the gas processing plant has been built in not many more months than there have been centuries in the growth of the village, and the plant now occupies an acreage not much less than the village. A great deal of time is spent by country planners and landscape architects and engineers in negotiating the siting and alignment of lines of power and communication, a necessary process, but one which, in large parts of the rural regions, draws attention away from more fundamental changes taking place in the landscape.

The landscape bequeathed by the eighteenth- and nineteenth-century landowners to their twentieth-century successors was predominantly one of small fields enclosed by hedges and trees, and interspersed with woodland and great parks developed on the estates of the aristocracy and, later, round the country houses of rich industrialists. Geoffrey Clark described the completion of the making of the landscape in a reference to ' . . . the nineteenth century—that heyday of the landowner, when from the fifties to the seventies, farming prospered and so many of the great farmhouses were built, which still appear in our landscape almost like castle groups. It was this period, too, when the final phase of enclosure took place which brought our landscape into its modern form . . . the rural England (they) produced was intact almost to 1914.'[59] This landscape is gradually being removed, particularly from lowland areas of intensive agricultural production. The reasons underlying the change are primarily agricultural —new techniques of cultivation, new crops and mechanisation—and technical, in the fields of transport and communications in the wider sense, but they also derive from changes in land ownership. The gentry of the eighteenth and nineteenth centuries laid out their estates in the firm belief that generations of the privileged few would continue to own them. Geoffrey Clark has described the rise and fall of the landowners' landscape in a succinct paragraph:

They studied their ground, they laid out their farms, they planted their wind-breaks and their coverts, they afforested their hillsides, they rebuilt, or kept in good order their ancestral homes surrounded by those magnificent parks and wonderful kitchen gardens, bothies and stable buildings. On that pattern our countryside was moulded. In thirty years the whole of this has departed and two world wars and high taxation has destroyed the continuity of this existence and the incentive to pursue long-term policies. In its place we are busily creating the welfare state and in the countryside trying to substitute for the owner-planner the Council and the Committee.[60]

The twentieth century has seen the political power of the private land-owner reduced and partly replaced by state and local government authorities and boards—the nationalised industries, regional boards and local councils whose corporate powers in respect of their own function usually exceed those of the individual. A vast acreage of land in the rural regions is held by—or on behalf of—the public, and is administered by boards and committees supported by a professional bureaucracy, professional both in its permanence and its membership of the architectural planning, land agency, surveying and other professional institutes. The Countryside Act, 1968, places on such public organisations an obligation to 'have regard to the desirability of conserving the natural beauty and amenity of the countryside' and 'to have due regard to the needs of agriculture and forestry and to the economic and social interests of rural areas'. That it should be necessary to require this regard for the country-side by law is perhaps a reflection on the extent to which government departments and boards can evade the policies and requirements local planning authorities would normally apply in considering development by private concerns and by district councils. (There is a procedure for consultation with local planning authorities, but no obligation on the part of the Government to heed the planning authorities' views.)

The twentieth-century contribution to the rural landscape varies from the vast operations of bodies like the Forestry Commission, who have planted many thousands of acres of forests, to the relatively small-scale extension of villages—mainly by estates of modern village villas—round an old and sometimes well-preserved centre. To the railway and canal have been added the motorway and electricity pylon. From the older pattern of field and hedgerow, miles of hedge and thousands of trees have been removed, particularly in the lowland rural regions, leaving an open and rather featureless landscape. It is surprising that there is not a more vociferous opposition to what is being removed from the landscape as well as to what is being introduced, new or as replacement. It is true that there are local groups—and some national ones—advocating rural preservation, but while these groups have strong lobbies in Parliament and on some local councils, they are supported by only a small section of the rural community, while the majority appear indifferent to (or unaware of) the destructive forces at work. The reason for this may lie in the insidious nature of rural change, a hedge rooted out here, a line of trees felled there, a line of pylons here, a new main road there; the mind soon adjusts to the new, though usually less pleasant visual scene, and change is accepted stage by stage which would probably provoke the most violent outcry if it were all carried out at the one time.

II. J. Lowe, County Planning Officer of Nottinghamshire, advocates district planting schemes supported by local councils. 'Our forefathers spent much time and money in creating a pleasant countryside embellished with trees and hedges. This landscape is fast disappearing, but there is no reason why a new and attractive landscape should not replace the old. Local Authorities, as successors to the old landowners, should take positive steps to create new beauty by setting aside a sum of money on an annual basis for tree-planting in rural districts.'[61] A wider view of the landscape needs to be taken than is evidenced in the preservationist attitude of many local councils and planning authorities. Some planning authorities have taken a comprehensive look at their rural landscapes though few have yet managed to evolve equally comprehensive plans or policies. Most planning authorities accept the facile and almost irrelevant division into areas of outstanding natural beauty, areas of high landscape value, and the remaining areas of open country. This division draws attention to the areas of finest landscape, and, until the recent Countryside Act extended the grant system, defined areas to which grants in aid of 'amenity' tree-planting and some other amenity provisions were to apply. But it does little to recognise or guide the major changes in the landscape. There is an urgent need for a study of the rural landscape to determine where changes are occurring on such a scale that comprehensive landscape plans are needed, and to recognise other areas where the older pattern seems to be surviving and to decide whether this situation is likely to continue.

However attractive the older landscapes of the eighteenth and nineteenth centuries may have been, and however attractive the remaining parts may still be, there seems little hope of, or sense in, trying to preserve it except in very special places, where it has a quality equivalent to buildings listed as of historic or architectural significance. Indeed, some similar list might be attempted for parkland and other high quality landscapes. Elsewhere, however, the case for resisting change is less and the forces of change will be even more irresistible. The 'Technology in Conservation' Study Group No. 3 of the 'Countryside in 1970' conference, noted that

modern arable farming requires larger farms for efficient mechanical cultivation, and the removal of hedges with internal field divisions of post and wire fences. Remaining hedges will be cut mechanically and will be of tidier appearance. The result will be a partial reversion to the more open fields of the period before the enclosures and the opening up of new vistas in the future. . . . There will be a large replacement of farm buildings of increasing size for intensive special enterprises and of tall silos. There will be an increasing use of prefabricated construction . . . farm buildings of the future will . . . be more prominent features of the landscape; they will be less frequently located in valleys and their siting poses many problems.

The economic forces behind these changes are too strong to resist successfully, even if resistance had any sense in it. A positive view of a future landscape in which aesthetic and agricultural and economic needs can be related will be of much greater value than any concept of widespread preservation. The newly formed Countryside Committees operating in most counties should resist the temptation to become official preservation committees aimed at defending lines of hedgerow trees which, if not already half dead of disease or old age, mostly stand in indefensible positions. Although there will be many cases where the preservation of trees will be justified, the attention of the committees would be better directed towards the planting of new, rather more than the preservation of old trees, and this applies not only to the open countryside, but also to the towns and villages of the rural regions.

It is hardly necessary to say that there are considerable regional differences in the way the landscape is changing, and therefore in the type of landscape plan needed in different rural regions. The removal of tree cover has been much greater in areas of intensive agricultural production than in areas devoted to animal husbandry. The opening out into a prairie landscape is a greater problem in East Anglia than in the pastoral lowlands of, say, the south-west of England, while the impact of poorly-aligned power lines or badly planned forestry is far greater in the hilly areas of, say, Northumberland or the Lakes than in East Anglia.

It would be wrong to give the impression that nothing at all is being done about the landscape problem. More refined methods of landscape survey are being developed, and some efforts have been made to replace lost trees and hedgerows; some landowners have planted new shelter belts, particularly where soil erosion or game rearing gives some incentive; there have been planting schemes for screening engineering works such as electricity sub-stations or sewage-disposal works; many highway authorities now plant trees near new roads, especially where land has been acquired surplus to requirements, but the chance and fragmented ownership of land does not provide a very satisfactory basis for the landscape architect to practise his art, and the general standard of planting schemes has not been particularly high, in spite of plentiful advice from many directions.

Although reference was made to the changing scale of agricultural operations and to the problem of siting new buildings in the landscape (including the interesting suggestion that some method of aesthetic evaluation be devised akin to economic cost-benefit), the Countryside in 1970 conference had little positive to say about the rural landscape problem, either about the destruction of the older landscapes, or the need for a new concept, designed to meet the requirements of a highly mechanised society, interested in quick movement, quick returns on low capital outlay and unrestricted flows of power. What is needed is a statement of aims against which to judge what is now happening and the power to promote long-term landscape plans and to guide other changes to fit in with them. The Countryside Act is a welcome move in this direction, but unless its implementation achieves considerably more than seems likely, it needs augmenting by further legislation requiring from various authorities more positive action.

An 'amending' Act should be introduced whereby:

(a) the Ministry of Agriculture, Fisheries and Food would be required to establish a department of landscape design, to co-operate with local farmers in schemes for improvement and modernisation of holdings;

(b) grant aid in tree preservation, and other tree-planting grants would be restricted to cover only schemes which were part of a comprehensive district landscape plan;

(c) the National Trust and Government Agencies would be required to prepare plans for landscape improvement and preservation for land under their control; the National Trust would be able to claim grants for landscape improvement in accordance with approved schemes;

(d) local planning authorities would be required to include in their plans, at an appropriate scale, proposals for landscape improvement in rural areas, in villages and in country towns. They would also be required to carry out detail planting schemes on land under their direct control.

8 Land and water resources and recreation

Town and country planning in Britain has been defined widely to include the task of protecting the nation's primary resources associated with the use and development of land and water. In this sense, primary resources include land for agriculture and forestry, land for surface mineral workings, land to be protected from building to safeguard the possibility of future underground workings, land for building and land for recreation; water resources include water for public supply or storage—for domestic, industrial or agricultural use, water for private supplies—usually industrial or agricultural, and water for recreation. A very large proportion of the land in the rural regions is devoted to agriculture and forestry, but mineral working and mining is also important in some regions, and building and recreational land needs can have considerable sub-regional and local importance.

The protection of land resources is achieved through the statutory powers and processes of the Town and Country Acts, administered mainly by the local planning authorities. In seeking the advice of the Ministry of Agriculture, Fisheries and Food about farms and farmland likely to be affected by development proposals, in making reservations of land for surface mineral workings, in preventing development where the threat of later subsidence might inhibit mining, and generally helping to secure a full and effective use of the country's natural resources, the local planning authorities act as direct agents of central government. This may be a convenient arrangement but it is one which raises some doubts, because the local planning authorities are equally charged with keeping a balance between social, aesthetic and economic aspects of land use, rather than the exploitation of any one.

Local planning authorities have a statutory duty to consult with the Ministry of Agriculture, Fisheries and Food, and the Ministry's Land Service will carry out agricultural significance surveys in areas where new development is likely, to indicate the size and boundaries of farms, the capital investment in terms of buildings and stock, the quality of land and the condition of buildings. With this detailed information to set against assessments of land need for other purposes, the Ministry of Agriculture, Fisheries and Food and the Local Planning Authority attempt to reach agreement on areas to be allocated for future development. In the case of larger towns, formal approval is obtained from the Minister of Local Government and Development, when a plan is approved as part of the County Development Plan. Plans for smaller towns and villages are approved by the local planning authority, without ministerial confirmation and agricultural land excluded from the planned development areas is therefore less formally protected—though not necessarily less effectively. The Ministry of Agriculture, Fisheries and Food has not sufficient staff to carry out significance surveys in every location in which development is proposed or anticipated and the preparation of many plans follows a hit and miss routine whereby areas of potential conflict with agricultural land preservation policies are recognised and the plans adapted until a compromise is found acceptable to both ministry and local planning authority, or a position of stalemate is reached.

Plans agreed with the Ministry of Agriculture, Fisheries and Food carry the implication that no agricultural objection will be raised when planning permission is sought for the development of land allocated in the plan. However, a development plan, even when formally approved by the Minister of Local Government and Development, is only an advisory document and does not commit the Ministry of Agriculture, Fisheries and Food to concede the land for building, either immediately, or at any future occasion. In practice, development in accordance with an agreed plan is seldom opposed. However, a more anomalous position may arise over the development of land not allocated on a plan: land may be omitted from a development plan solely on account of its high agricultural quality, on the advice of the Ministry of Agriculture, Fisheries and Food, and yet its development may be unopposed by the Ministry if a planning permission is sought as a departure—or variant—from the plan. In other words, the Ministry of Agriculture, Fisheries and Food may not sustain formal objection to the development of land which they have earlier advised the planning authority to exclude from the plan.[62]

Farming and farming techniques are largely outside the control, influence and experience of town and country planning and planners. However, the siting and design of large farm buildings is within planning control, and new barns, silos and other large buildings need the permission of the local planning authority. Control over single landscape elements even of this size hardly seems to justify the major administrative effort involved, or the results achieved. The worst designs may have been rejected, but not much has been achieved by way of positive improvement in the design or siting of farm factories, broiler houses and other large shed-like, semi-industrial structures.

The Ministry of Agriculture, Fisheries and Food gives grants for farm improvement, and can increase the grant to cover extra cost where these arise from amenity requirements.[63] In many cases the Ministry of Agriculture depends on advice from the local planning authority, especially where new buildings come within planning control. If the recommendation that the Ministry of Agriculture should establish a department of landscape design, is accepted, the Ministry could employ its own architects, and assume full responsibility for farm buildings as well as farm landscape.

On statutory plans, prepared under the provisions of the Town and Country Planning Act, 1962, agricultural land is protected only by being omitted from any development allocation, by being left in that wide tract of land 'where it is not intended that existing uses should be disturbed'. A more positive definition of the primary purpose of land as agricultural is foreshadowed in recent country management studies, such as that made jointly by Hampshire County Council and the Countryside Commission, in which the suggestion is made that planning, conservation and agricultural policies should be more closely related. It used to be maintained that planning is concerned with the protection of agricultural land, but not with the efficiency of its exploitation, or its particular agricultural use. In the words of Geoffrey Clark, in 1948, 'it is the first duty of all rural planning authorities to see to it that the maximum acreage of food producing land is reserved for agricultural occupation'.[64] Some country planners now find this concept too limiting, and wish to extend the function of country planning to guide the use of agricultural land, at least between a number of broad use zones. They wish to see greater interest taken by planners in the related development of agriculture and industry, to secure the economic support of the population of a farming sub-region. The development of the freezing industry at Great Yarmouth and Lowestoft is a good example of this type of development.[65] How far the town and country planner should become involved in the planning of agricultural land is debatable. His present function in advising between agricultural and other resource demands may be as far as he should go.[66]

F

R. E. Boote, Deputy Director of Conservation and Management in the Nature Conservancy, leading a discussion[67] on the Countryside in 1970, 'favoured emphasis on choosing the dominant use for an area, and then selecting those which might be compatible with it in varying degrees. This lessened the danger seen in some cases already of a secondary use claiming equality with what was clearly the best long-term use of the land.' By this means agricultural land might be indicated on development plans—at appropriate scale—in the same way as forestry land is now allocated, where the land is owned by the Forestry Commission, or where it is dedicated to forestry use under the Forestry Act. The present system whereby forestry land is allocated on statutory planning maps, but not agricultural land, seems the more strange because the planning authority plays a minimal role in the protection of forestry. Forestry controls are as much concerned with the capital invested as with the protection of the relatively poor quality land, and the wide powers vested in the Forestry Commission by the Forestry Act, 1963, are related more to timber production than to landscape conservation or to land resource preservation.

In spite of some anomalies, the protection of agricultural and forestry land through central and local government administration seems sensible and reasonably efficient, though how objectively the Government measures agricultural and forestry needs against development needs, and by what means, is less clear. The conflict between the demand for land to meet residential and industrial needs and the need to protect land as a basic agricultural resource has continued in one form or another for many years. Just before the last war, in the 1930's, the needs of defence against attack on our shipping lanes was emphasised as a reason for maximum agricultural production; since the war the argument has turned more on the contribution agriculture can make to our balance of payments problem. In spite of the loss of farmland to development home agricultural production has increased substantially. In 1964 Professor Wibberley described the increase in productivity in agriculture in this way—'if agricultural efficiency stopped increasing year by year, the agricultural area within this country would have to be expanded by about 10 per cent to meet the increased demand for food resulting from the probable increase in purchasing power and the larger population in 1970'.[68] In other words the effect of loss of land can be offset by increasing productivity elsewhere, and to a lesser extent, reclaiming poorly drained and derelict land. It can also be limited by guiding development onto poorer quality land, and many thousands of acres of good quality land have been saved through the operation of statutory town maps and planning controls. Nevertheless, there are economists who are not convinced of the need for this aspect of planning control, even on the grounds of maintaining a high level of home food production. Good farmland is often saved only at the expense of greater costs in other directions—in the provision of services and facilities for less well-sited development, and higher building costs in higher density development. No firm criteria have been established by which to decide the relative merit of, for example, developing on poorer land in poorer locations or developing in better located areas on higher quality land. Cost-benefit techniques are not easily applicable because of the great difficulty of costing the capital value of a difference in agricultural land quality to set against the different costs of construction, and against differences in the cost of providing and maintaining the basic services, roads, sewerage and transport. On the other hand the supply of land is a fairly fixed commodity—there being a limit to land reclamation —and the law of diminishing returns must set an upper limit to the extent to which land loss can be offset by increasing the productivity of poorer quality land.

A great deal of the argument about the preservation of agricultural land stems from the report of the 'Scott' Committee on land utilisation in rural areas, and most of that report was prepared before the second world war, when Britain was effectively an island, threatened from Europe and still recovering from acute economic depression. Thirty years have passed and a re-appraisal of planning policy towards agriculture is probably overdue. The case for the preservation of farm and forest land is strong, and the control of development is justified round the larger and expanding towns where the conflict between development and agriculture is greatest. However, in many parts of the rural regions the rate of new development is so low that, outside areas of first-class land, it is uncertain whether the results justify the cost of operating the machinery of agricultural consultation and control.

Mineral resources present to the country planner a somewhat different problem to agriculture. With agriculture, the problem is to protect land so that it may be used in perpetuity; with minerals, exploitation means a degree of despoilation, and the protection of land because it contains minerals has to be balanced against the problems which might be associated with their extraction. However, mineral resources are limited and potential demand has to be carefully assessed before permission is granted for development which would sterilise mineral deposits or before permission is refused for the exploitation of minerals from specific areas of land.

By far the greatest amount of mineral working, both surface and deep mining, is located in the conurban regions, but the rural regions contain significant mineral deposits, some of national significance. The ironstone workings round Corby, the granite workings of the Lakes, China clay pits in Cornwall, and brick clays in Hunts and Peterborough, are examples of large-scale mineral workings of national economic importance in rural regions. Generally on a smaller scale of operation, but far more widespread in distribution, are sand and gravel pits and lime pits serving local needs. Most minerals in the rural regions are worked on the surface, there being few mines outside the conurban regions.

In the control of surface mineral working, local planning authorities generally recognise the different problems posed by minerals of high value, or restricted location (and supply), and those of more general distribution and lower relative value. With high-value minerals, the local planning authority has normally to balance the need for the resource to be exploited—and this may have national economic significance—against the effect the workings may have on the local landscape and on local traffic conditions, a balance which is usually weighted heavily in favour of economic need. In the rural regions, landscape objection to the exploitation of high-value minerals (or those where resources are strictly limited) are only likely to be successful in National Parks and designated Areas of Outstanding Natural Beauty, and even in these areas, the case against exploitation has to be very strong.[69] With most high-value mineral deposits, potential for restoration is seen mainly as a means of ameliorating the effect of the worked-out pit, or scarred granite cliff rather than as a factor in deciding whether or not to permit the workings; but it is seldom that restoration, by filling or by planting, cannot be achieved at a cost within the means of the industry.

By contrast, with low-value minerals, the local planning authorities are moving towards a policy of allocating land for mineral working where a use can be found for the worked-out pit or where the land can be restored without too much difficulty. Where reclamation is impossible or too costly, dry pits may be developed as open spaces and flooded pits may be used for water recreation. The extraction of sand and gravel for building and engineering works is widespread and there is usually a choice of economically workable deposits within the economically viable distance of the areas of demand—in rural regions, mainly the larger urban centres, nearby conurbations and major road developments, in the very areas where recreation facilities are most needed, or most easily accessible to the majority of people.

Transport costs are a major factor in the location and operation of mineral workings. For example, the high cost of transporting crude iron-stone influenced the decision of Steward and Lloyds to establish a new steel works at Corby, a decision which eventually led to the designation of the New Town. Transport costs normally limit sand and gravel working to within 20 miles of the area from which the demand arises, while cement works are generally located on the chalk or limestone deposits. The high transport cost factor limits the extent to which a planning authority can prevent the exploitation of minerals; there is also a limit to the extra cost the public is likely to bear to prevent a mineral working in an area of beauty. High transport costs also mean that the exploitation of the mineral usually involves the erection of plant for grading and washing sand and gravel, and for the manufacture of cement.

Estimates of demand for minerals are made both by the industry and by the Government, through the Ministries of Public Building and Works and Fuel and Power.[70] There are no corresponding estimates of supplies or resources, and local planning authorities are therefore not usually in a position to judge objectively and effectively between economic and aesthetic or social priorities. There is not sufficient information available to either the authorities or the industry to make the most objective selection of sites, and the industry is not fully meeting its obligation to the community by continuing to operate without the benefit of more comprehensive surveys of deposits, including their location, depth and quality. In 1954, an Advisory Committee defined areas thought to contain workable sand and gravel deposits,[71] and many of these areas were allocated on statutory development plans for future mineral workings; a number have proved to be of no real value, although development for other purposes has been held up for many years to protect the deposits they were thought to contain. A more thorough and detailed investigation of sand and gravel deposits is being carried out by the Geological Survey on behalf of the Ministry of Public Building and Works, whose responsibility it is to safeguard the national interest in mineral workings. A comprehensive survey covering the whole field of mineral working would aid both the industry and the planning authorities, and would assist the central Government in deciding between the two in cases of disagreement that become planning appeals. Nevertheless, there is a high degree of co-operation between the industry and the planning authorities. Proven deposits of ironstone, chalk and limestone, the latter two used for cement manufacture on a large scale, special grades of sand used in steel and glass manufacture, and other minerals of national economic importance, are protected by development plans—and attempts are made to deal with the problem of land restoration rather than to limit production. Where minerals of national economic importance are concerned, no building or other development likely to prejudice their exploitation would normally be permitted, either by a local planning authority, or by the Minister of Local Government and Development on appeal to him.

In the 24 years of operation of planning under the Town and Country Planning Acts, 1947 (and its variants in the Acts up to 1962), planning decisions on surface mineral workings have been dominated largely by the economics of production; the object of most mineral operators is to produce a high standard of product, at low cost, to maintain a reasonable level of profit in a competitive market. Some operators also take a serious view of their social and aesthetic responsibilities, and certainly the operators associations take a responsible view of the future use of the worked-out land. Nevertheless, there are operators who seem to be out of sympathy with both the local planning authorities and their own associations, and for these a strongly expressed policy on the location and restoration of mineral-bearing land is needed and once approved by the Minister of Local Government and Development, it must be fully supported by the Government.

There is an increasing demand on rural land by recreational interests, to satisfy the needs of an increasingly mobile population, both from the conurban and rural regions. A 'day in the country' is a recognised prescription for lessening the tensions of city life, and the exodus from the conurban regions during summer weekends bears testimony to the general belief in the effectiveness of the cure. How far the desire to escape from the city reflects the paucity of the urban environment, and how far it represents a deeply-felt desire to re-establish contact with a more 'natural' one is unclear, and probably irrelevant, but many townspeople look on the countryside as a heritage which is theirs to share with the people who live in it—just as country people share the heritage of the historic centres of towns and make use of urban facilities. The countryside has not yet been fully organised to meet the needs of the urban population for recreation and leisure, and many landowners, farmers and foresters still fear the intrusion of large numbers from the conurbations. This fear has some justification, but in public utterance by landowners and agricultural associations it is often so exaggerated that each weekend one imagines hordes of marauders pressing on regardless, through fields of corn, trampling all before them, stopping only to leave open gates, light a few fires whenever they reach forest or woodland, and resting some distance away to watch cattle running amok in the barley, a pall of smoke rising gently in the distance. Nevertheless, with an increasing and increasingly mobile population, intent on using their motor cars for pleasure as well as for their daily routine travel, conflict in the countryside will be avoided only if provision is made for recreation and leisure in the right places in sufficient amounts. Areas of open country have formed a complementary part of most theories of urban growth, whether from the traditionalist pen of Ebenezer Howard or from the nouveau cite school of Le Corbusier. These open spaces have taken various forms—green belts round and defining the town, green wedges thrusting into the heart of it, or zones of horticulture to provide the urban population with local produce. Planned areas of open country are generally related to towns within the conurban regions and are not directly the concern of country planners working within the rural regions. However, as new concepts of conurban form are replacing earlier ideas of urban growth, the country areas which define and contain the conurbations will probably become the boundaries between the conurban and rural regions. Within these intermediate areas new demands are likely to be made for recreation areas, partly to resist residential and industrial development by delimiting it, and partly to satisfy the requirements of the Countryside Act, 1968, for such facilities as country parks. These parks are to be designed to provide large areas (25 acres or more) for formal and informal recreation in a countryside setting within reasonable distance of the major centres of population or where special features, such as water, give the areas a special attraction, like the Lakes or the Broads.

The rural regions contain most of the areas of exceptionally high quality landscape (the main exceptions being the Peak, which is within the

Midland conurbation and the Downs, which are in the London and
South Coast conurbation) (Map 16). The National Parks and Access to
the Countryside Act, 1949, was designed to secure the management of the
finest scenic areas, balancing between the general interests of the public
and the particular interests of farmers and other residents. The national
parks are a great success and in them considerable progress has been made
in solving the problem of how to give access to land without causing too
much disturbance to agriculture and other landed interests. However,
most of the national parks are on moorland or in mountainous areas
where the land is not intensively cultivated, if at all, and where there is a
very high proportion of permanent pasture and forest. The national parks
are comparatively large, the smallest (the Pembrokeshire coast) being
225 square miles. Areas not considered large enough to be parks, or where
it seems inappropriate to administer them through Boards or Joint Committees, have been designated as areas of outstanding natural beauty, a
designation which confers a status on land, and allows the local planning
authority to adopt a strongly preservationist policy and to obtain grants
to improve amenities. Like the National Parks, Areas of Outstanding
Natural Beauty are mainly within the rural regions, on coasts or in hilly
or downland areas.

The most popular tourist areas are the coasts, major inland lakes and
waterways, hill and moorland, many of them remote and well away from
the inland and lowland areas of intensive agricultural production. There
is little conflict between the holiday and agricultural industries because
there is little direct contact between them, and where they do come into
contact, it is mostly in the areas of hill farming or poorer land where
holidaymakers may provide the source of a welcome supplementary
income.

The demand for holiday accommodation is increasing annually, and
has been doing so for many years. By far the greatest proportion of the
increased demand has been for self-catering chalets, caravans, cottages
and boats. Large parts of the coastline have been pepper-potted with
holiday development, mostly caravans and mostly at very low standards
of layout and design. In small numbers, grouped informally round a large
open space, or set in trees, the caravan is acceptable and small static and
touring caravan sites should be provided in coastal and lakeland areas.
But in vast numbers, set out in rows, whether spaced according to model
standards or not, they make a dreary setting for a holiday, they give little

privacy and the open space round each caravan (needed as a fire pre-caution and to prevent direct viewing into the next caravan) is of little use as an amenity or for recreation. The chalet provides a more acceptable alternative. It is not much more costly to build, it gives greater privacy, and can be laid out more attractively round pleasant and useful open spaces. It can be provided with better sanitary facilities and running water, and, because it is built of semi-permanent materials and has a fixed loca-tion, it gives the site owner a greater incentive to invest more in roads, parking places and amenities. It also provides the local authorities with a greater rate return, which justifies the expenditure on sewerage, and the roads needed to give access to the holiday areas.

There is some indication that the advantages of the chalet over the caravan are appreciated by the holiday industry. Some caravan sites are being redeveloped with chalets, and chalets are being built on new sites. The industry is giving more attention to achieving a higher standard of accommodation and design and this improvement is by no means over-due. Some local planning authorities have adopted policies aimed at the replacement of the caravan by the chalet, but while this is a step forward, it is not sufficient without supporting policy on layout and design. Much recent chalet development has repeated the pepper-pot grid of the caravan layout. In all areas proposed for large-scale holiday development, local plans should be prepared, to show the basic pattern of layout, circulation and space, including provision for pedestrian and vehicular separation—to give safe and direct pedestrian access to the beach, especially for children.

Increasing demand for accommodation and its provision on a large scale, has meant a shrinking of the open coastline, and a call for the preservation of the remaining open stretches of coast. Through the National Trust, large sections of coast are being purchased for preserva-tion and the Countryside Commission (then the National Parks Com-mission) organised a series of regional coastal conferences at which coastal problems and policies were discussed. Most County Councils accept the need for coastal preservation but face a choice, between restricting the further spread of holiday development in any form along the coast and accepting it, and guiding it into more intensive forms. Chalets, and flatlets in 2 or 3 storey blocks—or higher—can replace low density caravan and chalet estates by a capital intensive form of develop-ment which is cheaper, more convenient, and of a generally higher standard. Accommodation might include the whole range from the all-in holiday camp to the individually-owned apartment, which is let by the owner when not using it himself; experience in existing holiday areas suggests that the larger and better holiday development will be largely self-supporting in facilities and that a fairly large township—of not less than 10,000 persons is needed if a town centre is to be provided for people staying in individual properties and in the smaller developments.[72]

The encouragement of intensive development in selected locations and restrictive policies elsewhere would mean both the preservation of the greater part of the open coastline and its enjoyment by larger numbers of people, both holidaymakers and day visitors. The implementation of this type of coastal policy may require some financial contribution from the national exchequer; alternatively, the holiday industry should contribute more to meet the overall costs of providing services; local authorities in the rural regions should not be expected to subsidise the recreational pursuits of a largely conurban population.[73]

The majority of holidaymakers in Britain seek accommodation on the coast, in the resorts, or in holiday camps, or on chalet or caravan sites. The resorts, with their hotels and boarding houses have not expanded at the fast rate that has characterised the holiday camp and chalet/caravan site side of the industry, and many resorts look towards a most uncertain future. Their heyday was at the beginning of the century, when the railway dominated in the field of long-distance passenger travel and holidays away from home were very much the prerogative of the well-off middle class. As yet, only some 60 per cent of the population take a holiday away from home each year, but this proportion is still more than double the number earlier in the century. Little of the increase has been accommodated in the resorts, although caravan and chalet sites accommodation has been provided on the slightly cheaper land nearby. Faced with an uncertain future, because of holidays abroad and because holiday development has spread along the coast, the coastal resorts are seeking new forms of enterprise. The marina, the covered entertainments centre and similar large scale enterprises requiring capital expenditure in the order of two to three million pounds, are designed to overcome both the vagaries of the weather and the comparatively short season common in coastal towns. Whether the capital will be forthcoming to implement these proposals and what degree of success they would have in attracting more visitors over a longer season is uncertain, but the holiday industry is becoming more and more competitive and the resorts will have to demonstrate their ability to meet this competition if they are to assure their own future.

Within the rural regions there are inland areas of considerable attraction as recreation centres, in the National Parks, and in hilly, moorland or mountainous country (Map 16). The Lakes and Dartmoor are probably the best known and the most popular. The Norfolk Broads also attract large numbers of people, the attraction in this case being the waterways rather than the scenery, which although distinctive, is rather dull.[74] In each of the main inland holiday areas, overcrowding is probably the most serious problem. Conflicts between various recreation uses—e.g. fishing and boating—and between recreation and other interests (e.g. boating, nature conservation and water extraction in Broadland) are also difficult problems. In each area there is considerable scope for improved management, for bodies with the power to manage the conflicting interests and to implement the proposals of the local planning authorities. In the national parks, these could be park boards; elsewhere they might be specially constituted authorities.

A more specialised recreation need is that for organised sport. Organised sport is changing as people turn away from team games, which require not much more than a pitch and some changing rooms, towards individual sports, with more specialised requirements, such as swimming, sailing, fishing, water-skiing, golf, badminton and athletics. Schools are encouraging individual sports more than in the past, and demand for facilities is likely to continue to build up. Large expanses of water for boating or water-skiing are not easily found, and sports halls, running tracks and swimming pools are costly. In the future, recreation facilities are likely to be provided in the larger towns, or where there is a convenient stretch of water.

Land is the major resource of the rural regions, whether exploited for its agricultural quality, mineral content or scenic value; the rural regions also contain most of the nation's water resources, and water is an important rural resource, for which four primary users compete—the great conurban populations, and their industries; the local population and industry; agriculture, mainly for irrigation; and the riparian users, including port authorities and sporting interests who require a sufficient level and quantity of water to be left in the rivers. In some rural regions there is already conflict for water, and there is considerable potential demand, which could lead to further conflict unless additional supplies are developed. The Water Resources Board published a report in 1963 on the need and potential supply in each region, and in a series of sub-regions.[75] It is clear that the demands from the conurban regions are likely to be met from the water resources of the rural regions, although the capital required for the development of the source and the storage of the supply is likely to come mainly from the conurbations, either as their share of tax revenue, or more directly through local Water Boards. Reservoirs built in hill areas, to hold winter water for summer supply, affect less agricultural land. Nevertheless, they usually provoke considerable conflict when first proposed, because they usually involve drowning whole farms and sometimes even hamlets. Water must be provided for the large conurban populations in increasing amounts, and it will be sought from the nearest reasonable sources of supply; thus, for example, the construction of a pumping main from the Ouse catchment to North-East Essex, and the development of more resources in North Wales to serve Merseyside.

From this short review of rural land and water resources, it is clear that there is little fundamental conflict arising from their exploitation. Generally, intensive agriculture is well away from holiday areas or potential reservoirs, or mineral workings. Where conflict occurs in the rural regions it is generally a fairly localised affair, concerning problems of access, land restoration, the use of surface water, the design of holiday development, and the impact of exploitation on the landscape.

9 Problems, objectives and research

Country planning is prone to suffer from periods of fashion. The contribution of agriculture to rural society, the impact of urban society on rural life and village planning, are examples of subjects which have had periods of popularity. It is as if planners sought light relief from their more acute urban problems, in the relative simplicity of the countryside. At present, attention is focussed on rural resource planning and conservation, and these subjects seem to have drawn rather too much attention away from the more intrinsic problems of settlement, employment and population.

In the rural regions there is a clear distinction between planning to meet demand arising from the conurban regions, and planning to improve the environment and the opportunities for the resident population. In recent years, and particularly in the studies associated with the Countryside in 1970 conferences, rural planning has been seen largely in terms of the countryside meeting the demands made upon its land by the conurbations. The hard-core problems of unsatisfactory settlement pattern, lack of local employment opportunity, poor facilities, and the destruction of the rural landscape in intensive farming areas are not receiving sufficient attention.

Four problems dominate in the planning of the rural regions, two arising from the needs of the resident population, the third related to links between the rural and conurban economies, and the fourth concerned with the exploitation of resources, mainly for the conurban populations:

(1) The settlement pattern is outdated—Professor Wibberley has called it archaic—and no longer serves adequately the needs of the rural population. It needs to be recast in a form which recognises and reflects social and economic changes and in particular, the increasing mobility of the population, the higher standards of living and education, and the greater range of facilities, opportunities and services expected by those who dwell in the country. There are too many villages, which, by any measure of cost against benefit, are too small, and many larger villages and small towns no longer seem to be viable economically or socially because they need larger populations to support their shops, schools and other social and commercial institutions. Even round the somewhat larger towns,

where there has been growth, this has not been very selective and, despite
the operation of the planning Acts, plans for schools, shops, industry and
public services have not been, and still are not, fully related to residential
development. Although the local planning authorities are also the education, highways and health authorities (in the counties) and the housing
authorities as well (in the County Boroughs) they still act as if they are
four or five different organisations, so strong is the entrenched system of
committees in local government. It is sometimes more difficult for a
planning committee to negotiate with another committee of the same
council than to negotiate with another authority or private developer.
The rural building and development programme needs to be rationalised,
and a stronger form of rural planning authority is required. The provincial councils and unitary authorities, proposed by the Royal Commission on Local Government in England, would provide larger and
more effective planning authorities, which would share the responsibility
for planning the structure and distribution of settlements, but they might
still lack sufficient executive powers in the rural regions.

(2) Country planning has had comparatively little effect on the physical
environment of the countryside, in spite of the wide powers of planning
held by local planning authorities over the past twenty years. It has
inspired little change that would not otherwise have taken place, and its
effect on what has occurred has been marginal. A large part of the change
in the local environment in the countryside is outside the scope of
planning control, but those changes within the control of the planning
authorities have been less than satisfactory. This may be due to the volume
of material that planning committees have to consider, but it is also a
reflection of the quality of planning committees and their advisers. Plans
which have been prepared for towns and villages either remain no farther
advanced than when first drafted, or have been implemented in the
private sector so far ahead of the public, that there is a strong suspicion
that the plans are unrealistic in over-estimating the likely expenditure in
the public sector of the economy. Development plans and development
control policies in the rural regions, while indicating the possibilities of
long-term improvements, fail to recognise the limited scope for positive
achievement.

(3) The level of activity in the rural regions, in building and engineering operations, in agriculture, forestry and recreation is increasing in
scale. This is largely to meet the increasing demands of the conurban

populations, to pass through, or carry the products of their work through the rural regions, or to pass their leisure time in the rural regions. Most forms of economic organisation are increasing in size, and it is difficult to equate this larger scale of activity (and the problems it poses in the siting of motorways, power lines, factory farms, holiday camps, vast mineral workings, large reservoirs and similar large-scale development in the rural landscape) with the traditional and largely preservationist view of country life, in country town, village, hamlet and farm.

(4) Conurban demands on rural resources—for minerals, water supplies, and land, and water, for recreation, holiday accommodation and for the products of farm and forest—are greatly increasing. There is a strong case for meeting these demands, and generally rural interests are not sufficiently strong to withstand them. The Stanstead airport proves the exception to the rule, although in that case the opposition seems simply to have managed to move the demand for land from one agricultural location to another. The problems posed by the exploitation of rural resources generally go far beyond the technical and financial capacity of the local authorities in the rural regions. The proposed 'unitary' authorities would be stronger financially, and would be able to employ better technical assistance, but they might still require aid from central or provincial sources. Alternatively, a greater contribution to local affairs might be required from resource industries, particularly agriculture.

The nature of these four problems, and the extent to which they occur, varies between and within the rural regions. Proximity to—or remoteness from—conurban areas, and the distribution and extent of the contrasting growth and decline areas, make a considerable difference to the type of problem, and to the form of plan and policy needed to cope with it. Nevertheless, there are aims and objectives which are common to all rural regions.

The primary objective in any rural plan is to secure changes in the pattern of settlement that will increase the range of social, commercial, and public services, and educational and employment opportunities, and make them available to a greater proportion of the resident population. In the words of R. L. Stirling, 'our development plans should be based not so much on repopulating the countryside as on providing all those services which are needed for the present population—to give them parity with the townsfolk'.[76] (An echo here of the Scott Committee's belief that parity in services might cut back the drift from the land.) This increase in facility and opportunity will normally be achieved by increasing the populations supporting the social and business life of the major towns and villages, either by attracting a population increase from outside the area or by effecting a redistribution of the existing population at its present level or even less. Again in the words of R. L. Stirling, 'If we plan principally to assist the development of services needed by the existing population there are certain manifest influences which affect the form and content of that plan. Generally they are influences tending towards concentration and a revision of the pattern of rural settlement.'[77] Limited economic resources and the very considerable capital already spread out in small villages and hamlets set a practical limit to what can be achieved, but the future standard of living in the rural regions will depend in some measure on the extent to which migrational movements (into and within the regions) and the exercise of control over the location of new development can be turned to good account. A full life in the country increasingly seems to mean life in larger country towns and larger villages on the main lines of inter-urban communication. In more practical terms the aims of rural settlement policy were outlined in the *Analysis of the Survey for the Devonshire County Development Plan*, published in 1964, as:

(a) provide the best environment for the countryman;

(b) encourage the setting up of new activities and sources of employment in the country;

(c) secure the most economic distribution of public utilities including gas, water, electricity, sewerage, telephone, postal services and social services such as schools;

(d) make an adequate system of public transport services in rural areas a practical objective;

(e) preserve the rural landscape for the countryman and holidaymaker;

(f) maintain a convenient distribution of readily accessible village centres, particularly in areas of rural depopulation.

The report then suggested that the best way to achieve these aims was 'by ensuring that major extensions of residential development and public utilities are only permitted in selected key settlements', but it seems doubtful whether this policy has very much hope of succeeding unless backed by something more positive than guiding the location of new development; new development must be attracted in the right quantity to selected places, by economic incentives, by overspill schemes, and by other economic and social policies. The Hunt Committee on the Intermediate areas accepted the need for minor growth locations in the rural regions, but believed they would grow of their own volition. The Economic Planning Councils generally support both the continued growth of the larger towns and cities in the rural regions, and the selection of intermediate growth centres in the medium-sized towns. The Hunt Committee saw the choice in the more remote areas as between travelling 20–30 miles to work in an expanding employment centre, or moving to live in the centre. The local authorities generally find this proposition unacceptable, and see the need for a greater number of centres, more widely dispersed. In mid-Wales, the Government has accepted the proposition of small town growth with the expansion of Newtown by a Development Corporation, but in England the policy is different, and the Government seems to look unfavourably on this use of the New Towns Act. Nevertheless, studies are being made to assess the need, and to establish criteria for the selection of growth centres of different sizes.

With new town and town expansion schemes already under construction and some well on the way to completion—it might be expected that a method of selection had already been developed, based on established criteria which could be adapted to the general rural situation. However, town expansion schemes were largely the result of political decisions by local councils to take advantage of the provisions of the Town Development Act, to help solve their own local problems. The location of the expanding towns was not the result of any comprehensive study or of the application of any objective planning criteria.

The Economic Planning Councils' reports include suggestions about possible growth forms, but because of the definition of the regions, these are more concerned with conurban than with rural regional growth. The main exceptions are East Anglia and the South-West; East Anglia is wholly rural in the sense in which rural is used in this book, but the East Anglia Study is a rather disappointing document, so far as growth forms for rural regions are concerned. The Study simply recommends that future growth should continue to be concentrated into the four main centres of Norwich, Cambridge, Ipswich and Peterborough (Cambridge in spite of the Local Planning Authority's restrictive policy aimed at protecting its historic centre) with subsidiary growth at the largest of the many small towns in the region. The problems of a population dispersed into too many small settlements are capably, if rather superficially, discussed, but no remedy is proposed apart from a vaguely stated belief that it will be enough to maintain the smaller market towns at about their present size by industrial development aided, where necessary, by some form of grant. In their rival *Appraisal*, the Local Planning Authorities' East Anglia Consultative Committee suggest that this weak acceptance of the trend in the growth of the major centres, and a statement of pious hope for the remainder, will not solve the rural problem.

The Committee is preparing a regional strategy, and this may offer a more positive solution to the region's problems.

In the Ministry of Housing and Local Government's Bulletin on *Settlement in the Countryside*[78] it states that 'Within the framework of regional policy, a wide range of choice is open to planning authorities in deciding the future of settlements. The feasibility of alternatives must be tested against programmes of public investment and the costs balanced against social and economic benefits.' Sound enough advice, but limited against a background of unclear regional policy, and ill-defined methods of selection. (Lack of advice on the possible forms of rural development—or retrenchment—reduce considerably the value of the Bulletin. Generally, there appears to be no guidance from Government quarters on criteria for selection of growth locations, either in their numbers or in their distribution.)

There are few locations which are physically unsuitable for development, and the criteria for selecting development locations in the rural regions are therefore mainly social and economic. Development at selected locations should achieve four main objectives:

(1) A fuller utilisation of under-employed capital assets, such as roads, public services, schools and other facilities; alternatively, where facilities have to be provided, growth should be at a scale whereby these facilities can be provided most effectively.

(2) The concentration of traffic movement onto a limited number of primary road and rail routes, into which all available funds would be directed: the definition of primary routes would take account of the total funds likely to be available.

(3) The correlation of programmes and plans for various forms of development, including hospitals, schools, shops, roads and public services.

(4) A viable programme of employment growth or redistribution, based on industrial or commercial enterprise, where necessarily stimulated by financial and other incentives.

The application of these criteria will depend, in practice, on the amount of existing capital commitment, and on the likely future rates of development and investment. Planners in the rural regions have looked on population and employment trends, and the rates of house-building and industrial development, as reliable indicators of likely future investment levels and have based town and village plans on them. In some cases, not only the rate, but also the location of new development has been 'planned' to follow past trends, whether or not the trend is improving the settlement pattern overall. The reluctance to plan against the trend is understandable: local planning authorities have extremely limited powers to implement a plan which proposes any change in the rate of economic growth, or the level of investment in any particular direction, or in a population trend. Sometimes the more audacious authority allows its plans to become tinged with a little faint optimism, and a bid is made for a somewhat higher rate of growth than the trend suggests.

How seriously can local planning authorities be expected to plan for comprehensive changes in the settlement pattern in rural regions, when even in the growth areas, the rate of development does not appear to be sufficient to achieve any very considerable change with a normal long-term planning period of between, say, 15 and 30 years? Potential for change varies from region to region, from area to area, but even in the more remote parts of the rural regions there is a rate of development and a scale of population movement which, *taken together*, mean that a worthwhile measure of change could be achieved. If full advantage can be taken of residential mobility, it should be possible to effect a 50 per cent change in the physical pattern of settlement every 30 years, by the combined effect of economic incentive (differential rating to cover the extra cost of servicing the remote locations is one possibility) and strict planning control once the future pattern had been decided. In political terms, a 30 per cent change in 30 years would be a substantial achievement. In practical terms, the opportunities for change will be greater in growth areas than in areas where the population is declining or static. In growth areas, selected for major economic growth, or where there are large commuter or retired populations, change is likely to be achieved by the growth of some places relative to others; elsewhere changes are likely to be achieved only by stimulating growth in a very few places at the actual expense of the others, and that is the price the whole area would have to pay to retain any level of economic viability. Apart from some movement of retired people into country areas, the future of the rural regions rests primarily with economic policy, and a decision at Government level whether rural communities should be subsidised. Although the larger towns and cities in the rural regions have succeeded in attracting some new employment in both the manufacturing and the service sectors of industry, the rural regions as a whole are at a considerable disadvantage compared with the conurbations. Present economic policies and circumstances favour the conurbations and generally offer little to the rural regions. At present, there is nothing to indicate any change in policy on industrial location. Nevertheless, if it is decided that there should be viable country towns at intervals between the major regional and sub-regional centres, it is a legitimate function of country planning to promote industrial growth in areas where economic opportunity and social facility are too limited, and to suggest methods of achieving this objective. The difficulty facing country planners is that outside the main centres of population, the rural regions have attracted only the marginal industrial enterprises, small concerns seeking to develop where overheads are low, or the last units in the long line of branch works, the first to feel the effects of economic recession. It may be that there are small to middle-sized industrial enterprises which are not mere offshoots of larger firms which do not need their markets on their doorstep or an immense pool of labour, and which could operate successfully in the rural regions, should they be given the incentive to do so. If subsidy is thus required to promote industrial growth, it is the price the community has to pay to maintain a tolerable level of services for the agricultural population of farmers, farmworkers and their dependants who will continue to live on the land; the alternative is to allow the majority of country towns to be replaced by the larger towns or nearby conurbations, as shopping, education, employment and entertainment centres.

Viewed comprehensively, local authorities' plans for the rural regions add up to not much more than a combination of individual town maps, designed to accommodate the trend in each town (or some slight variation in it) and key village policies whereby villages are generally classified into those suitable for expansion, less suitable for expansion and not suitable for expansion. To these largely unrelated plans for the location of new development are added allocations of land for particular purposes, such as mineral extraction or landscape preservation, and a definition of a major communications and transportation network. The need to relate these plans to a more comprehensive regional and sub-regional pattern is generally accepted but before effective plans can be prepared for the rural regions comprehensive studies need to be made of growth forms applicable to the rural regions and of the economic capacity of these regions to support various patterns of settlement, in relation to both the rate of potential industrial development and to the level of future investment. A Rural Studies Group should be established to sponsor and, where necessary, carry out research in planning and allied subjects in the rural regions, in conjunction with the research departments of Universities and other institutions. The terms of reference for this group should include:

(1) Changes in the settlement pattern and forms of growth most appropriate in rural regions and sub-regions, taking account of varied economic and social circumstances.

(2) Levels of investment in industry, commerce, transportation and communications, social and public services, needed to achieve planned changes in settlement pattern and in relation to particular forms of growth.

(3) The application of cost-benefit techniques to show how to secure from rural development the highest return in social facilities, employment opportunities and public services for the least capital outlay in both the public and private sectors of the economy. (The study of various forms of growth round Norwich by the University of East Anglia is an example of the type of work needed in this field.)

(4) In conjunction with the Ministry of Technology, industry in the rural regions, its location, materials, lines of supply and communication, labour supply and markets and in particular the possibility of introducing new industry into those areas where limited employment opportunity suggests that lack of support population may jeopardise the future of towns providing services for the rural population. The Small Towns study being undertaken by the East Anglia Economic Planning Council and Consultative Committee is a start in this direction.

10   A planning framework for the rural regions

The experience of planning and other authorities in implementing plans in rural regions—particularly where these involve the introduction of new industry into the smaller country towns in the more remote rural areas—shows that the level of investment in industry, commerce and transportation is generally lower than that needed to sustain the existing level of services and employment. It will be a major task to initiate schemes of rural development or to guide development into the right place at the right time. A rural authority is needed with both administrative and executive planning and development powers. The executive powers would include the development of industrial sites, the building of advance factories, the construction of roads, housing for key workers, and the provision of some social and public services. The Authority would administer a rural development fund, to which both local and central government would contribute. The fund would be used to finance development carried out by the Authority, and would provide for grants, which the Authority would be empowered to make towards the cost of industry, housing, communications and transport in areas defined as being in special need. These special areas would be subject to confirmation by the Minister of Local Government and Development. The idea of a rural development authority is not new. The rural industry boards had a few of its suggested functions. Ray Pahl suggested in 1964 that 'possibly some areas should be more positively planned by a sort of rural development corporation'.[79]

It is quite unclear what the present Government intends at a regional level of administration. If no change is made in the present system of Economic Planning Councils, if Councils are established for provinces as defined by the Royal Commission on Local Government in England,[80] or if some other form of regional organisation is adopted which does not distinguish between rural and conurban regions, the rural development authorities might be *ad hoc* bodies, each covering a rural region. The members of the authorities would be drawn from the local authorities in the region, and from the economic planning, or provincial, councils. But to achieve effective planning in the rural regions, the provinces should be defined to distinguish between rural and conurban regions, and to create some form of rural and conurban provincial councils.[81] The provincial councils for the rural regions would then become the rural development authorities, and would be given any additional powers necessary to administer and use their development funds. The Royal Commission suggested that provincial councils should 'have a reserve power to undertake development necessary to ensure the success of a provincial plan'.[82] In the rural regions, these powers should not be held merely in reserve.

The Royal Commission also suggested that provincial councils should 'settle the provincial framework of land use and economic strategy within which planning authorities (in the unitary areas) must operate'. The provincial plans would establish a pattern for settlement, industry, employment communications and transport. This pattern would be translated into both the formal structure plans which local planning authorities have to submit to the Minister of Local Government and Development for their areas, and the local plans dealing with specific localities. The local planning authorities would be required to consult the provincial council during the preparation of their formal structure plans, and the provincial council would be required to advise the Minister of Local Government and Development on plans prepared by local planning authorities. In practice, plans for the rural regions might be prepared jointly by provincial councils and planning authorities. Where the provincial council and the local planning authority failed to agree, the Minister of Local Government and Development would arbitrate, and where this procedure failed, the decision would rest with the Minister.

The provincial councils would also be concerned, with the local planning authorities, in the exploitation of resources in the rural regions. Together, provincial councils and local planning authorities would be charged with the responsibility for achieving a balance between local interests in, say, preservation, and the wider regional or national interests for which any particular development is required. At present, Local Planning Authorities are inclined to attach more importance to local than national or regional views, and the influence of the provincial councils should help counterbalance this bias.

The plans prepared under the 1947–62 Acts were multi-purpose documents, bringing together into one set of maps and statements, proposals and policies relating to various subjects. The Town and Country

Planning Act, 1968, brings into formal planning the concept of different plans for different purposes, a concept of particular value in rural regions where a clear distinction needs to be drawn between plans for the resident population, its settlement pattern, housing, transportation and other services, and plans for the exploitation of resources and for the development of recreation facilities, where the need may arise from outside the rural region and demand may be subject to seasonal variation.

Structure plans will need to be prepared for a variety of subjects, but these will normally include: the settlement pattern and transportation; recreation; resources; and communications. The general content of these plans is described briefly in Appendix 2.

These four basic, regional and sub-regional, rural structure plans will represent the main physically identifiable parts of the system of social and economic activities, and the changes envisaged in the system by the provincial councils and local planning authorities. The plans will need to be based on an analysis of the operation of existing social and economic activities, and the changes which are taking place in both the system and its operation. In conurban regions, the pattern of economic and social activity is intensive and complex; by contrast, the pattern of activity in rural regions seems simple, but extensive. Nevertheless, both the system of activity and communication linkage are sufficiently involved to justify study in some depth, and for this purpose a comprehensive survey will have to be made requiring more advanced and refined methods of data collection and processing than have been used by most local planning authorities in the preparation of development plans in the rural regions. Few local planning authorities have shown a willingness to face the expenditure involved in adopting advanced survey and analytical techniques (indeed few planning committees have ever been advised of the need to do so), and for this reason, and so that both the equipment and the skilled staff may be shared, a statistics and research unit should be established to serve each rural region. This unit would be financed from the proposed rural development fund and would advise Government departments, provincial councils and local planning authorities on existing social and economic conditions and trends, and on the likely impact of new major development proposals on the operation of the system. The unit would operate a data bank, develop the use of computer techniques, and cost-benefit and other methods of comparative analysis in town and country planning in the rural regions.

The new Planning Act requires that greater attention shall be paid to the economic viability of plans. The more efficient the proposals, the more will be achieved during any particular 'plan period', and tests will need to be applied to various plan possibilities to discover the plan with the highest cost effectiveness, particularly in the public sector. In practice, cost effectiveness tests are made by assessing the capital cost of public services and facilities including roads, sewers and schools, and comparing the loan charges on these capital items with the rate return expected from any related development. To do this, local planning authorities require the services of valuers and quantity surveyors, professions which are seldom represented in planning departments in the rural regions, although most departments already call on other departments for valuation and costing advice. The volume of this work is likely to increase considerably, and a specialised unit should become part of the provincial council's organisation. Otherwise the local planning authorities will have to engage their own experts in this field.

A close tie-up between transport and physical planning is required under the Town and Country Planning Act, 1968, and under the Transport Act, 1967. The fragmented ownership of the major bus companies has been replaced by the National Bus Company and joint boards will operate in the major conurbations. In planning in the conurban regions, transportation policy is directed largely towards persuading people to travel by public rather than private transport to ease the congestion on the roads. In the rural regions this policy is only necessary in the largest regional centres or where the historic character of a town may be endangered by heavy flows of traffic, and the road proposals that would be needed to deal with them. More usually the problem in rural areas is to find a way of retaining a public transport service sufficient to meet even the most basic needs of the population, to reach school or shops in nearby towns. There will need to be the closest co-operation between the provincial councils and the transport operators, and the councils should be empowered to subsidise rural services from the rural development fund.

The successful application of new techniques and of the new structure plans envisaged in the 1968 Act, to the rural regions, will depend on the quality, education and training of local planning authority and provincial council staff, and on the quality and imagination of councillors. There has been an encouraging movement of well-trained planners from the Universities into Local Planning Authority planning departments in the rural regions in the past few years but there is a pressing need for the more senior officers to keep up with the new thinking and the new techniques.

The emphasis in planning, and in the allocation of funds for development is rightly towards the conurban regions, and there is little left for the rural regions; nevertheless, the rural regions may expect to see some considerable improvement in the scope and quality of country planning, including:

(1) A realistic set of regional, sub-regional, district and local plans, closely related to the operation of the social and economic system.

(2) Plans capable of implementation within some reasonable period.

(3) A clearly stated set of objectives aimed at improving the level of social and economic facilities and opportunities for a fuller life in the rural regions.

(4) Plans which will not appear—as at present—as a finite article to be achieved by means of specific proposals, to be carried out within a fixed period, but as a series of objectives to be achieved by a series of related actions, each part of an endless chain of events, and each a contributory part of the system.[83]

One of the more serious criticisms of planning is that the control of development, which is achieved at the cost of both delay and inconvenience to people wishing to develop land, has become too much a matter of administration and too little concerned with planning objectives and the implementation of physical plans. In the future, it is hoped that planning control in the rural regions will be related to established and generally understood and accepted plan objectives. A new and more positive view of development control is needed in which it is seen as part of the social and economic system and not something apart from it. In this way there should be less emphasis on administrative procedures, and more emphasis on the achievement of positive improvements in the rural environment.

It is recognised that there are neither the skills nor the resources to change quickly from the methods of the 1947 Planning Act to those of 1968 and beyond. For this reason the structure plan part of the 1968 Act is to be brought into operation by stages in a few areas at a time. The Government has announced the first eight areas in which the new type of development plans might be introduced, subject to the agreement of the local planning authorities, and it is encouraging to see that one of these areas is wholly within a rural region (Map 17). Apart from this area, it must be accepted that the rural regions are likely to follow the conurban regions in the application of the new Act. Most of the thinking so far applied to the new Act has been related to the conurban problem, and further study is needed before effective structure plans can be prepared for rural regions. It is hoped that this book will aid in these studies.

It is clear that what is most needed in rural planning is the recognition of the fundamental difference between the conurban and rural regions, between their problems and the policies needed to solve them, between the scale of economic and social activities in each, and between the probable investment levels in their future development. Positive planning achievements have been largely in the conurbations, and the development of new planning techniques have been oriented largely towards the conurban problem. This does not detract from the 'preservationist' achievements of rural planning authorities, but it is significant that those major signposts in the development of planning in the past 10 years, *Traffic in Towns*,[84] the Planning Advisory Group Report of 1967,[85] the 1968 Act, and the latest studies into the application of mathematical models[86] and systems planning, have been largely concerned with conurban situations. Rural planning still relies on the techniques devised in the late 1940's for the implementation of the 1947 Planning Act. Where new planning techniques have been introduced they have been adapted from conurban planning, and technique and theory directly applicable to the rural regions, and to the limited staff and funds available, have yet to be developed.

The majority of people in this country live in the conurbation regions. They look to the rural regions for some of their food supplies, for much of their recreation and for a place to retire. They travel through the rural regions in comparatively large numbers from one conurbation to another. The conurbations are overcrowded—the rural regions are relatively under-populated: the rural regions could accept people from the conurbations and in this sense their planning could be complementary. The planning problems in the rural regions are neither so acute nor so pressing as in the conurbations; nevertheless, a substantial minority of some eight million persons live in the rural regions of England and Wales, in a large number of towns and villages, the future of some of which seems to be in doubt. At the threshold of new opportunities in town and country planning it is important to see that country planning is not again left behind; it is only sensible that we take stock of the assets of the rural regions to conserve what is best, to build anew where opportunity occurs and offer those who choose to live away from the great centres of trade and industry, the fullest life that their circumstances may allow.

In planning the rural regions, a balance needs to be struck between the needs of the resident population and the exploitation of resources. In practice, these are likely to come into conflict at a local scale, and possibly in some rural sub-regions. There is likely to be little conflict on a regional scale. Nevertheless, planners considering the future role of the rural regions sometimes assume that growth (which may be of great benefit to some towns and villages) will conflict with the rural roles of agriculture, forestry and recreation. This assumption has little foundation within the rural regions.

Areas of high agricultural value generally lie away from major recreation areas, and there is sufficient poor land clear of both to allow development which would not conflict with land conservation policy to any serious extent. Nationally, and regionally, the resource interests are well represented through the Ministry of Agriculture, Fisheries and Food, the Ministry of Public Works and Building (minerals) and the Countryside Commission (recreation). The interests of only some groups of local residents are well expressed, through organisations such as the Country Landowners' Association and the National Farmers' Union (both with vested interests in the exploitation of resources). Local Government has failed to speak with a sufficiently loud and coherent voice on behalf of the resident population it represents. In many parts of the rural regions, it is dominated by sectional land-owning and farming interests. The Government might consider it worthwhile to sponsor an investigation into the role of the rural regions, their needs and potential.

The expanded towns programme in the East of England and south-central England rural regions, shows that some part of the economic growth of the expanding conurbations can be hived off to small towns. Even if the town expansion programme represents an insignificant proportion of conurban growth, it can be very significant within the rural regions. The difficulties involved in planning growth too far from the conurban centres have been stressed on a number of occasions, and recently Dr Burns and his team have made the point yet again in their study of alternative strategies for the south-east.[87] It is said that the south-east can accommodate its own growth, but this should not preclude consideration of small town expansion schemes in the adjoining rural regions, where these may bring some local benefit. The good sense which seems to have prevailed in Wales should be extended to the rural regions of England.

The conurban regions are likely to be extended at the expense of the rural (Map 2), but even within the remaining rural regions, and in the transitional zones, there will remain scope for selective expansion and growth. Without any major conflict with rural resources, there is scope to expand many towns, and to increase the population of the rural regions. The role of the rural regions should be to offer an alternative place of residence and work to the conurbations, as well as to meet primary resource, and recreation needs. A full life in the country should be a reasonable prospect for an increasing number of people.

Appendix 1 Mobility in the rural regions

A. Personal and daily mobility
Sources:
   Village Life in Hampshire, survey carried out by Hampshire County Council and Mass Observation Ltd., Hampshire County Council, Winchester, 1966.
   Kent Development Plan: Quinquennial Review, 1963, 'Report of Survey and Analysis', Part 4, Vol. 1. 'Mid-Kent Employment and Shopping Survey', Kent County Council, Maidstone, Sept. 1964.
   First Review of the Cambridgeshire County Development Plan: report of survey, Cambridgeshire County Council, Cambridge, 1965.
   Surveys for village development plans published by Oxfordshire County Council: *Adderbury Social Survey*, 1967; *Burford Social Survey*, 1967; *Goring Social Survey*, 1965.
   A. R. Emmerson and Rosemary Crompton, *Suffolk: Some Social Trends*, report to Suffolk Rural Community Council, University of East Anglia, Norwich, 1968.
   Norwich Area Transportation Survey: Interim Report, Norwich City Council, Norfolk County Council and Ministry of Transport. Norwich City Council, Norwich, 1969.

The Hampshire study, based on a sample survey by Mass Observation Ltd., contained the following general conclusions:
   (1) One-third of the people worked in their own villages, just over a third in towns, and the remainder in the countryside or villages other than their own ... most of this movement to work was local in character, half the journeys out of the village being less than six miles long. Among the 16–24 age group, 85 per cent travelled out of their own village to work, mainly to towns. 75 per cent of managerial, professional and skilled manual workers travelled out of their village to work whereas in the clerical, supervisory and unskilled manual groups the proportion was a little over half.
   (2) Sixty per cent of respondents (to a questionnaire) went out of their village to shop once a week or more often, mainly to a nearby town; three-quarters of the journeys to shops were less than eight miles long; there has been an increase of about 5 per cent in the number of shopping trips outside the village during the past five years, presumably facilitated by increasing car ownership.

(3) Seventy-five per cent of respondents sometimes leave their village to visit friends and relatives elsewhere; 40 per cent of these do so at least once a week; younger people and the managerial/professional occupation groups made more visits than did the other groups.

(4) Taking the average of all days in the week, about half the respondents left the village on each day. Proportionately, many more young people went out than old people. The journeys were mainly short in both distance and time. A third went to nearby towns, about a third to more distant towns and a third to other villages or places in the countryside.

(5) A table in the report indicated that 73 per cent of all journeys were made by car, compared with 17 per cent by bus, 5 per cent by cycle and 1 per cent on foot. Of the journeys made by males, 81 per cent were by car and only 9 per cent by bus, while of the journeys made by females, 62 per cent were by car and 28 per cent by bus; of journeys made by people over 65 years of age, 40 per cent were by bus and 51 per cent by car.

'Mid-Kent Employment and Shopping Survey', based on sample selected from an area within a radius of about fifteen miles round Maidstone, mainly within a rural region, but close to the London conurbation: two extracts from the report of survey summarise the findings about mobility, as follows:

(1) In the southern part of mid-Kent, '63 per cent of all workers were em-ployed in their own village or hamlet or in some other part of the area. A further 22 per cent worked in Maidstone and an area within 15 miles of the centre of the area.' The other parts of mid-Kent showed 'differing degrees of dependence on the local area for work—in mid-Kent (west) the proportion was 75·7 per cent, in mid-Kent (south-west) it was 54·8 per cent, in mid-Kent (east) 56·8 per cent and in mid-Kent (north) 26·0 per cent. All these areas showed the influence of Maidstone to some extent; approximately 26 per cent of workers from mid-Kent (north) and (east) were employed in Maidstone and 20 per cent from the south-west area.'

(2) Maidstone dominated much of the mid-Kent rural area for luxury shopping, the other three principal urban areas being virtually self-sufficient for all types of shopping. For weekly shopping, Maidstone's area of influence was smaller than for luxury shopping, extending approximately eight miles from its centre; even so, the rural areas tended to be self-sufficient for daily and weekly shopping, using Maidstone as a secondary centre for the latter.

Cambridgeshire report of the survey for the first review of the County Development Plan, a survey also based on the replies to questionnaires; for the survey, the County was divided into five main areas of residence, the City, the immediately adjoining villages, and villages in two further rings round the City and in an outer area. The survey indicated that:

(1) Eighty-seven per cent of the residents in the City also worked there and only 7 per cent regularly travelled to work in the remainder of the County or beyond.

(2) From the adjoining villages, 49 per cent travelled to work in the City, 31 per cent worked locally, and 11 per cent travelled to other parts of the County or beyond.

(3) Travel to the City from the two middle rings and from the outer villages decreased with distance, the proportion being 30, 20 and 4 per cent respectively. Just about half the local working population from these three areas obtained employment locally, while between 15 and 30 per cent travelled to work in the remaining parts of the County outside their own particular (survey) area.

(4) Town dwellers generally journey lesser distances to work than do villagers; how far this is generally applicable to towns and villages in rural regions is not certain, but the Cambridgeshire pattern of employment being concentrated more in the town than the surrounding villages is widespread, and the journey to work pattern is likely to be common to many areas.

(5) Tables were included in the Cambridgeshire Report showing where people did their day-to-day and weekly shopping. 'The outstanding feature of these tables is the very high proportion of total shopping trips which are purely local—in the suburban centres, in the case of the City residents, and within the same village in the rural areas. Even for the main weekly shopping an appreciable proportion of trips are local. . . . Within the rural areas the larger villages are to a considerable extent self-supporting for household shopping, while the smaller ones tend to make much greater demands on Cambridge and the other towns.'

Oxfordshire village studies, carried out by the local planning authority, give specific examples. In Adderbury, a village 4 miles from Banbury, 56 per cent of a total working population of 840 travelled daily to work in Banbury, while only 23 per cent worked in the village. Fifty-nine per cent travelled to work by car, while only 14 per cent normally walked to work. A high proportion also travelled regularly to shop in Banbury. In contrast, in Burford, a village some 12 miles from Oxford, there was less commuting, 65 per cent of the working population of 460 being employed locally, and 17 per cent within the Rural District. Only 21 per cent normally travelled to work by car, and 6 per cent by bus. A high proportion shopped locally for foodstuffs, but a substantial number also made regular trips to shop at Witney, Oxford or Cheltenham.

University of East Anglia survey of East Suffolk rural districts, carried out by the School of Social Studies, gave the following information about mobility (based on a sample):

(1) Forty-nine per cent of working adults included in the sample worked in their own village, 23 per cent worked in towns in East Suffolk, and 7 per cent worked in towns elsewhere in East Anglia. The remainder worked in rural districts, but outside their own village.

(2) All people in the sample were asked why they normally visited 'town'; 72 per cent said for shopping, 9 per cent said for work, 7 per cent said for leisure and 5 per cent said to visit friends or relatives.

(3) The frequency of visits to 'town': at least once a day 8 per cent; more than twice a week 10 per cent; about once a week 25 per cent; more than once a month, less than weekly 28 per cent; more than once in three months, less than a month 10 per cent; rarely, a few times a year 13 per cent; and the remainder 2 per cent.

(4) Location of leisure time activities: home centred 42 per cent; village based 31 per cent; town based 29 per cent; and others 12 per cent.

The results varied with the location of each village, and particularly with the distance from Ipswich.

'Norwich Area Transportation Survey', based on a 10 per cent sample of families resident in the built-up area of Norwich, with a population of 170,000 persons. A total of 257,000 were recorded during an average 12-hour day, from 7 am to 7 pm (a further 203,000 trips were made in returning home).

(1) Trip purpose: journey to work 32 per cent; journey in course of work 7 per cent; journey to school or other educational institution 14 per cent; journey to shop 21 per cent; journey for social reasons 6 per cent; and journey for personal business 20 per cent.

(2) In the morning peak, 38 per cent of journeys were to work, and 41 per cent to school. In the evening peak, 52 per cent were from work.

(3) Eighty-four per cent of trips originated at home, and 16 per cent from elsewhere. Ten per cent of journeys to work were to destinations outside the built-up area, while during the day, 300,000 vehicles entered the built-up area, nearly 70 per cent of these being private cars.

(4) Of the total 460,000 trips (including those to return home) nearly 40 per cent of those in Norwich were on foot, 31 per cent were by car or motorcycle, 16 per cent were by bus and 12 per cent were by cycle. Of worktrips, 28 per cent were by car, 20 per cent by cycle, 19 per cent by bus and 17 per cent on foot. Sixty-three per cent of trips to educational institutes were on foot. Fifty-four per cent of trips to shops were on foot, and 46 per cent of trips for personal business were on foot.

H

(5) Ninety-five per cent of bus users stated that they had no other form of transport available.

(6) Car ownership: 43 per cent of families had 1 car, 6 per cent had two and 0·4 per cent had 3 cars.

Nearly half the families had no car.

B. *Residential mobility*

Sources:

Ray Pahl, *Urbs in Rure, a survey of villages in Hertfordshire.* Geographical Paper No. 2, London School of Economics, 1964.

'Two villages in North Norfolk', a study by County Planning Dept., *Planning Outlook* No. 1, University of Newcastle, Dec. 1966.

Kent Development Plan: Quinquennial Review, 1963, 'Report of Survey and Analysis', Kent County Council, Maidstone, Sept. 1964.

Village Life in Hampshire (see Appendix 1A).

Goring Social Survey (see Appendix 1A).

Suffolk: Some Social Trends (see Appendix 1A).

Urbs in Rure: a survey showed that in two commuter villages in Hertfordshire, only 20 per cent of the men, and 10 per cent of the women were local, while in a nearby agricultural estate village, only 35 per cent of the chief wage-earners were locally born.

'Two Villages in North Norfolk' showed that only 50 per cent of the adult population resident in the two villages in 1951 was still there in 1961. Some had died, but the majority had moved away on change of job, or marriage or retirement. They were partly replaced by people reaching the age of 21, or by people moving into the villages, but the net migration was only about one-fifth of the gross.

The mid-Kent survey found that the proportion of people who had moved into the survey area between 1951 and 1964 varied between 35 per cent and 40 per cent.

Village Life in Hampshire: 26 per cent of residents had lived in their village for less than 5 years and 40 per cent for less than 10 years.

The study of Goring revealed that nearly half the families had moved into the village between 1955 and 1965.

In the East Suffolk rural districts study, the length of residence in the villages was given as follows:

Years	%	By individual district %
less than 5	22	15–33
5–9	13	12–16
10–19	18	12–21
20–49	33	26–37
60–69	10	8–13
70 or more	5	1–13

The place of birth of village residents was also given: 21 per cent were resident in the village of their birth; 26 per cent were born in rural Suffolk; 11 per cent were born in rural districts of East Anglia; 14 per cent were born in urban areas of East Anglia; 2 per cent were born in rural districts outside East Anglia; 13 per cent were born in urban areas outside East Anglia; and 10 per cent were born in London.

Appendix 2   Structure plans

Content of the four basic, regional and sub-regional, rural structure plans.

Settlement and transportation

The Settlement and Transportation plan is likely to include, for each rural region, proposals and policies indicating:

(1) Scale of industrial activity and growth, and the location of industrial and employment centres, related to the type of manufacture, its sources of raw materials and its markets, and the routes used by its transport.

(2) The anticipated future level of population, and the location of settlements or areas where large-scale housing development is anticipated.

(3) The location and function of centres serving the resident population.

(4) Major routes, indicating their function, and distinguishing between those used primarily to link conurban regions through the rural region and those providing a distribution system primarily for the rural region. The primary function of the rural regional routes should be indicated, together with some scale of anticipated use.

(5) Major public transport service routes, indicating the capacity and frequency of the intended service, and its function, e.g. general inter-urban, commuter, shopping, etc.

(6) The location of areas for which local plans are to be prepared, indicating the subject of the plan.

Recreation

The structure plan for recreation in the rural region should include policies and proposals relating to:

(1) The scale of provision of holiday accommodation, the form of accommodation and its approximate location; an indication will be given of the routes by which holidaymakers are likely to travel and anticipated peak traffic flows.

(2) The restriction of other forms of development because priority is to be given to holiday and other recreational interests; and the corollary—where specified recreation needs are likely to be met.

(3) The policies to be followed in areas of high landscape value, including Areas of Outstanding Natural Beauty.

(4) The location of areas for which local plans are to be prepared, indicating the subject of the plan.

Resources

Plans for resources in rural regions should provide for 'the effective integration of the many interests and agencies concerned with development, conservation and management, e.g. in agriculture, forestry, power, physical infrastructure etc. . . .' (Travis). The structure plan should lay down the framework for this, close co-operation between the planning and producing interests by indicating:

(1) The location, quantity and quality of mineral deposits of known economic viability and the anticipated programme of working.

(2) The location of other mineral resources and a programme of exploration.

(3) Areas where the policy will be to restrain development to safeguard agricultural production, forestry and water supply: a distinction could be drawn between those areas needing protection against anticipated development pressures and those areas where only exceptional proposals are likely to constitute any serious interference with agriculture.

(4) Lines of primary communication related to the exploitation of rural resources, including the routes by which primary products are 'exported' from the region, and including the distribution centres for agricultural products, markets and routes likely to be involved in heavy seasonal traffic flows.

(5) Centres intended to serve the agricultural and other primary industries, to provide specialised services, e.g. sales and service to farm machinery, and to provide for the day-to-day needs of the farming population and other people living in dispersed locations.

(6) The location of areas for which local plans are to be prepared, indicating the subject of the plan.

Communications

The Communications structure plan should indicate the pattern and intended operation of the passenger and freight systems:

(1) Air and sea services, indicating scheduled services by destination, frequency and capacity, for freight and passengers. Special services related to functions within, or beyond, the rural region should also be indicated.

(2) Main-line rail services, indicating the intended frequency and destination of passenger services, and goods facilities by the intended location of goods stations of varying types (e.g. liner services) and the surrounding area within which regular delivery and collection is to be maintained.

(3) Motorways and other main roads linking conurbations and rural regional and sub-regional centres.

(4) Main distributor road system, indicating the function of roads and where seasonal traffic flows are anticipated.

(5) The location of major traffic generators, including settlements, industries, resource and recreational areas, and indicating where the plans anticipate new or increased traffic generation, and in what way.

Notes

Chapter 1

[1] 'The Countryside in 1970' conferences, held in Nov. 1963 and Nov. 1965. and Oct. 1970. Reports of twelve study groups were published separately, as *The Countryside in 1970: Reports of Study Groups, 1965.* The following subjects were covered: 'training and qualification of planners'; 'training and qualification of professions concerned with land and water'; 'technology in conservation'; 'countryside planning practice'; 'review of legislation'; 'outdoor recreation—active and passive'; 'traffic and its impact on the countryside'; 'preservation of natural, historic and other treasures'; 'countryside planning and development in Scotland'; 'information and the countryside'; 'living and working in the countryside'; and 'reclamation and clearance of derelict land'. The Conferences were sponsored by the Council for Nature, The Royal Society of Arts and the Nature Conservancy.

[2] The population statistics were taken from the mid-year estimates for 1968, published by the Registrar General. The transitional zones between the rural and conurban regions generally lie across the boundaries of the sub-divisions of the economic planning regions, for which population figures were published in 1968. The sub-divisions within the rural regions are numbered and described in the quarterly returns, as follows:

North England rural region
3. Rural North-East: North.
4. Rural North-East: South.
5. Cumberland and Westmorland.
16. Furness.
17. Lancaster.

East of England (inc. East Anglia)
12. South Lindsey.
24. Northampton.
25. Eastern Lowlands.
31. North-East—East Anglia.
32. North-West—East Anglia.
33. South-West—East Anglia.
34. South-East—East Anglia.
38a. Beds and Bucks (part).
38b. Berks and Oxon.

South-Central England
38b. Berks and Oxon.
42a. North Gloucestershire.
42c. North Wiltshire.
43. Central South-West.

South-West England
44. Southern South-West.
45. Western South-West.

Wales and the West Country
30. Rural West Midlands
51. North-West Wales—remainder.
52. Central Wales.
53. South-West Wales.

Lists of the counties, and other local authority areas, within each statistical sub-division, are included in the report of the Committee on Intermediate areas, and the sizes of towns were taken from these figures. In some cases, such as Norwich, the built up area extends into adjoining rural districts, and the population figure is too low.

[3] The Town and Country Planning School, held annually under the auspices of the Town Planning Institute. The school is attended mainly by members and students of the Institute, but is also open to non-members, and attracts a few councillors and others interested in planning. There are usually five main papers, and a series of seminars and discussion groups.

[4] Lionel March, Assistant Director, Land Use and Built Form Studies, University of Cambridge, School of Architecture.

[5] The Royal Commission on Local Government in England (Cmd 4040), under the chairmanship of Lord Redcliffe-Maud. Its report, in June 1969, advocated the complete overhaul of local government, by the introduction of elected provincial councils, to replace the nominated economic planning councils, and large new unitary and metropolitan authorities, to replace the present county, county and municipal borough, and district councils. The metropolitan authorities would be in the major urban areas, where there would be a second tier of metropolitan district councils. The unitary authorities would function elsewhere, supported by local councils, whose main task would be the representation of local opinion.

[6] op. cit. paragraph 433.

[7] op. cit. paragraph 287.

[8] op. cit. paragraph 412.

[9] *The Reform of Local Government in England*, Government white paper, H.M.S.O., Feb. 1970, Cmnd 4276.

[10] *Wales—the Way Ahead*, Welsh Office, Cmd 3334, H.M.S.O., 1967.

[11] Where the national boundaries between England and Scotland, and England and Wales, run through a rural or conurban region, the regional or provincial council would have to look to the administrative centres of both countries. This would raise difficult problems of political control and responsibility, and rural provincial councils would have to work with central government departments in London, Cardiff and Edinburgh, and possibly in Newcastle. Plans would have to be submitted to the Minister of Housing and Local Government, and the appropriate Secretary of State, or which ever Ministers should replace them, if the relative status of the three constituent parts of Great Britain is to be changed.

[12] The concept of the 'sphere of influence', or 'service area' surrounding each town is discussed briefly in Chapter 6, p. 46, and in note 47.

Chapter 2

[13] An interesting parallel to the pattern of daily movement is to be found in the 'social network', as seen by Barnes, and quoted by Ronald Frankenburg in *Communities in Britain*, a Pelican Original, Penguin Books, Harmondsworth, 1966. Barnes wrote 'the image I have is a set of points some of which are joined by lines. The points of the image are people . . . and the lines indicate which people interact with each other . . . a network of this kind has no external boundary, nor has it any clear cut internal divisions, for each person sees himself as the centre.' If the home is accepted as the location from which people live their social and economic life, the links they have with other places—by indirect means, for example by telephone, or direct means, for example by personal visits—correspond with some of the lines described by Barnes. Important parts of the social and economic network follow physical lines of communication, and the daily mobility of people is a measure of a part of the system very relevant to planning.

[14] In preparing Chapter 2, reference was made to published survey material on mobility in town and country in the rural regions, including:

Village Life in Hampshire: Hampshire County Council and Mass Observation Ltd.

First Review of the Kent County Development Plan: Kent County Council.

First Review of the Cambridgeshire County Development Plan: Cambridgeshire County Council.

Village plan surveys by Oxfordshire County Council.

Survey of rural districts in East Suffolk by the University of East Anglia.

Norwich Area Transportation Survey: Interim Report: Norwich City and Norfolk County Councils, and Ministry of Transport.

Planning Outlook: a survey of two remote Norfolk villages in an article on remote rural areas.

Ray Pahl: *Urbs in Rure, a survey of villages in Hertfordshire*. See Appendix 1 for details.

[15] The use of mathematical models in planning has been developed by Lowrie, Crisp, Wilson and others in the past ten years. Much of the work of the Centre for Environmental Studies has been devoted to the use of models, and the recently published Notts.-Derby Study (*Nottingham and Derbyshire: sub-regional study*, Nottinghamshire County Council, Derbyshire County Council, Nottingham City Council and Derby County Borough Council, 1969) illustrates their application to a practical problem. They seem to have two different applications in relation to mobility:

(1) to give an estimate of the volume of movement likely to arise from a particular distribution of population, employment, schools, shops and other facilities.

(2) to give an assessment of the residential distribution likely to arise from a particular distribution of employment, schools, shops, etc.

The first group, known as trip generation models, are a means of testing plans for housing industry, etc. The second group carry the use of models further, to illustrate the possible result, in practice, of a series of planning policies or restraints. Mathematical models are likely to become a standard part of planning analysis.

[16] *Settlement in the Countryside—a Planning Method*, 1967, H.M.S.O. Planning Bulletin No. 8 Ministry of Housing and Local Government.

[17] See note 14 and Appendix 1.

[18] See Appendix 1.

[19] Most surveys of residential mobility include a question about the reasons for moving into the country; in the Hampshire survey respondents to a questionaire listed nearness to work in 34 per cent of replies, better or cheaper housing in 21 per cent, and to gain peace and quiet in 14 per cent.

[20] *The Report of the Committee of Inquiry into Land Utilisation in Rural Areas* (the Scott Committee), 1941, one of three major reports which had considerable influence on planning legislation between 1943 and 1947.

[21] David Thorns, 'The Changing System of Rural Stratification', *Sociologia Ruralis,* Vol. VIII, No. 2, Royal Van Gorum, Assen, Netherlands, 1968.

Chapter 3

[22] *The Analysis of the Survey for the Devonshire County Development Plan*, 1964.

[23] Large subsidies are payable for rural water supply and sewerage schemes. The cost of maintaining rural schools is spread over the whole of each county, and the standard charges for telephone, postal, and a number of other delivery services, means that urban services are subsidising rural. An interesting study of the costs of services in rural areas was published in 1969, following a comparative study between the cost of supplying water to a dispersed population, and the cost of supplying the same population concentrated into fewer, larger villages—*The South Aitcham Scheme—an economic appraisal*, 1969, H.M.S.O. The study covers the costs and benefits of relocating population, but it takes no account of what might be achieved by voluntary migration over a period of years, as it assumes that all families affected by the scheme would have to be compensated for moving to a larger centre.

[24] In Norfolk, 1952–1969, 62 primary schools were closed in rural areas.

[25] The effect of mobility on school location is discussed briefly on page 12.

[26] J. B. Ayton and the author, 'Changes in the pattern of Rural Settlement', paper submitted to 'Planning for the Changing Countryside' conference, Oct. 1967. Conference report published by Town Planning Institute. Copies available from County Planning Officer, Norwich.

[27] *Cambridgeshire and the Isle of Ely County Council Development Plan Review, 1968: Report of Survey*, Cambridgeshire and Isle of Ely County Council, Cambridge, 1968.

[28] These studies are quoted more fully in the research paper mentioned in note 26.

[29] Town and Country Planning School, 1966.

[30] R. W. Stirling, County Planning Officer of Lindsey County Council, speaking at the Town and Country Planning Summer School, 1953.

[31] *Rural Planning in West Suffolk*, West Suffolk County Council, Bury St. Edmunds, 1968.

Chapter 4

[32] Economic Development Committee for Agriculture, *Manpower in the Industry*, National Economic Development Office, H.M.S.O., Oct. 1967.

[33] *Employment and Migration in the Fakenham Employment Exchange Area*, Norfolk County Planning Department Technical Paper, 1970. Obtainable from County Planning Officer, County Hall, Norwich.

Chapter 5

[34] Peter Hall, Professor of Geography at Reading University.

[35] Peter Hall, *New Society*, January 1970, 'The Motorway Boom Ends'.

[36] *The Countryside in 1970*, 'Living and Working in the Countryside', 1965, see Note 1.

[37] *The Countryside in 1970*, ibid.

[38] *White Paper on Transport and Traffic*, 1966, Cmd 3057, H.M.S.O.

[39] See note 16.

Chapter 6

[40] *East Hampshire Area of Outstanding Natural Beauty: a Study in Countryside Conservation*, published by the Countryside Commission, Nature Conservancy, Ministry of Agriculture, Fisheries and Food, Forestry Commission and Hampshire County Council, Winchester, Oct. 1968.

[41] Town and Country Planning Summer School, 1950: Paper by Dr G. P. Wibberley, 'Changes in Agriculture'.

[42] *New Houses in the Country*, Ministry of Housing and Local Government, 1960, H.M.S.O. This expressed the view that, apart from agricultural dwellings, new houses should normally be located in villages rather than in the open country.

[43] *Rural Nottinghamshire*. Reports prepared by the County Director of Planning and published by Nottingham County Council, July 1966–May 1969. *East Retford Rural Districts*, July 1966; *Worksop Rural District*, Nov. 1966; *East Area*, March 1967; *South Notts.*, February 1968, and *Central Notts.* May 1969.

[44] Discussion on the 'New Village' at the Town and Country Planning Summer School, 1965, led by Andrew Thorburn.

[45] The report *The South Aitcham Scheme—an economic appraisal* mentioned in Note 23 may give a lead in this direction.

[46] R. D. P. Smith, Technical Officer, East Anglia Consultative Committee, 'Changing Urban Hierarchy', *Regional Studies*, Journal of the Regional Studies Association, Sept. 1968.

[47] In a prize-winning essay, 'The development of settlement form' (Town Planning Institute, 1967) Ruth Longworth states that 'in response to choice, patterns of behaviour seem to be changing and with them the functional relationships between magnets and their catchment areas. As information is assembled from the land-use transportation surveys on actual catchment areas, we begin to find many discrepancies with hierarchial theory . . . movement between home and other uses is more varied, more random and less predictable than most planners have realised. Mobility over greater distances for purposes of work, leisure, shopping, education and so on increasingly ignores hierarchial patterns.'

[48] *East Anglia—A Regional Appraisal*, East Anglia Consultative Committee, Bury St. Edmunds, Feb. 1969, Map A.

[49] In August, 1965, the mid-Wales Industrial Development Association recommended development at 5 centres, but a report by Economic Associates Ltd., commissioned by the Secretary of State for Wales, recommended the development of a single new town.

[50] The Secretary of State for Wales set up the mid-Wales Development Corporation and gave it, 'as its first task, the expansion of Newtown', which the consultants had recommended as part of their total Caersws project. In *Wales*, 1968 (H.M.S.O.) the Government reported that an outline plan for Newtown had been prepared and that they had accepted the feasibility of doubling the size of Rhayader. Discussions were taking place with County Planning Officers and the mid-Wales Development Association to select towns 'where the main effort to secure growth should be concentrated'.

[51] *The Intermediate Areas:* Report of a Committee under the Chairmanship of Sir Joseph Hunt, Cmd 3998, H.M.S.O., April, 1969.

[52] See note 48, and page 46.

[53] Discussed in slightly more detail on page 45.

[54] However, the County plan usually includes an overall estimate of population growth for some fixed period, up to 20 years, and its possible distribution, at least between the major towns and the rest of the county.

[55] The 1968 Act provisions about development plans are not yet generally in force; they are to be applied to individual authorities by 'commencement' orders. The recently published manual *Development Plans—a manual on form and*

content, 1970 (H.M.S.O.), gives a full description of the type and content of plans to be prepared under the Town and Country Planning Act, 1968.

[56] The example of Nottinghamshire has already been quoted, on page 41, and in note 43.

[57] Only the structure plans for the county, or large town, will be formal; the remainder will remain informal, although approved by the County Council.

Chapter 7
[58] Most Counties have agreements with district councils, delegating a wide range of development control powers. The district council is usually advised by a planning officer of the County Council, and when the planning officer and the district council cannot agree, the case is referred to the County for decision. In practice, the majority of applications are decided at district council level. An alternative procedure is to work through area committees of county and district council members.

[59] Geoffrey Clark, then Director of Planning, Devonshire County Council, in a paper 'The Planning Problems of Rural Areas', Town and Country Summer School, 1957.

[60] Geoffrey Clark, op. cit.

[61] Rural Nottinghamshire—I. East Retford, see note 44.

Chapter 8
[62] This anomaly arises from the different view taken by the Ministry of Agriculture, Fisheries and Food, of the preparation of plans for whole towns or villages, where large areas of land may be involved, and individual planning applications, which affect relatively small parcels of land. The acceptance of development on a small site may not be inconsistent with the preservation of a large area of farmland—of which the site is a part—but it gives rise to misunderstanding.

[63] *Farm Buildings in the Countryside*, a booklet prepared jointly by Ministry of Housing and Local Government, Ministry of Agriculture, Fisheries and Food, Welsh Office, Council of Industrial Design and Countryside Commission, H.M.S.O., 1969.

[64] 'The Planning of the Countryside', a paper by Geoffrey Clark, then Director of Planning, Devonshire County Council, at the Town and Country Planning Summer School, 1948.

[65] See pages 27 and 28 for a brief description of the impact of the freezing industry on farming in the surrounding area.

[66] In the East Hampshire study, the planner was one in a multi-disciplinary team, and he can make a successful contribution in this limited role.

[67] Town and Country Planning Summer School, 1966.

[68] 'The Changing Rural Economy of Britain', a paper by G. P. Wibberley, Town and Country Planning Summer School, 1964.

[69] The recent case of the potash workings in the North Yorks. Moors National Park is interesting in this context, and can be studied in the annual report of the Countryside Commission for 1969.

[70] Ministry of Public Buildings and Works Circulars, prepared bi-annually to cover two years, e.g. *Sand and Gravel Production 1963–1964*, H.M.S.O., 1965. *Sand and Gravel Production 1965–1966*, H.M.S.O., 1967.

[71] *Report of the Advisory Committee on Sand and Gravel* under the Chairmanship of A. H. S. Waters, H.M.S.O., 1954.

[72] 'Holiday Town', unpublished booklet, prepared by Norfolk County Planning Department, to which reference can be made on request.

[73] A recent study of the feasibility of holiday development along the Wash coastline showed that the rate return from intensive chalet development would not be adequate to finance the public works needed to support the development.

[74] A full survey of the Broads has been made by the County Planning Officer of Norfolk, for a consortium of local authorities. The County Planning Officer's report advocates both conservation and expansion in a plan which would cost over £10 million, shared between private enterprise and the local authorities—or a Broadland authority.

[75] For example, *Water Supplies in South East England*, Water Resources Board, 1966, H.M.S.O.

Chapter 9

[76] R. L. Stirling, 'How can a development plan assist rural development', paper presented to Town and Country Planning Summer School, 1953.

[77] R. L. Stirling, ibid.

[78] *Settlement in the Countryside—a Planning Method*, see note 16.

Chapter 10

[79] A discussion group led by Ray Pahl on 'Rural Communities', Town and Country Planning Summer School, 1964.

[80] See Chapter 1, pages 5, 6 and 7.

[81] See Map 5 and page 7.

[82] The Royal Commission on Local Government in England, paragraph 417.

[83] The concept of planning as part of the economic and social system, as well as a controlling factor, and the idea of the plan as a flexible set of objectives, which not only inspire but are also affected by every change in the system, is described generally as systems-planning, and is very clearly described by J. B. McLoughlin in his book *Urban and Regional Planning—a systems approach*, Faber and Faber, 1969.

[84] Colin Buchanin, *Traffic in Towns*, H.M.S.O., 1963.

[85] *The Future of Development Plans*, H.M.S.O., 1965, a report of the Planning Advisory Group of officers of local government, the professions and central government departments.

[86] See note 15.

[87] *South East Joint Planning Study: a Progress Report*, prepared by the South-East Joint Planning Team, 26–28 Old Queen Street, London S.W.1, H.M.S.O., Dec. 1969. The Report states that 'the team paid particular attention to their view of the strength of present trends, notably the tendency for the population of Greater London to decline and that of the outer Metropolitan areas to increase; to the short distances involved in transfers of many factories and offices out of London; and of the problem of the least skilled workers who appear not to have shared proportionately in the opportunities for workers to move away from London. . . .' The strategies being studied by the team contain no major element of growth in the adjoining rural regions, except what is already committed, mainly in the form of large New Towns, such as at Milton Keynes and Northampton and Peterborough.

The Reports of the Town and Country Planning Summer Schools are published annually by the Town Planning Institute, 26 Portland Place, London W.1.

In October 1970, as a result of a Government re-organisation, the Ministries, of Housing and Local Government, and Public Building and Works, were reconstituted as the Ministries of Local Government and Development, and Housing and Construction, within a new Department of the Environment. For publications prepared by the Ministry of Housing and Local Government, this title has been retained; elsewhere the new title has been adopted.

Index